MW01171781

HOLY
SPIRIT
ADVENTURES

God at Work in
the Marketplace

Jennifer Weiss

DOVE
PUBLISHING HOUSE

CONTENTS

ACKNOWLEDGEMENTS

I dedicate this book to my Lord, Savior, endless-pursuer, and lover of my soul, Jesus Christ. He knew me when, and He loved me even then. This book could never do justice to how much you love your people. Words are not sufficient to give You the honor, love and glory due.

I am grateful to my husband, Jonathon, who is my sturdy, strong leader. He does all the things good leaders do. He supports me, serves our family with absolute selflessness, and he bankrolled this book. Thank you, my love.

To our crew: Monica, Chad, JG, Carly, and Tanner, as well as to my beautiful granddaughter, Grace. You all have my heart and are a catalyst for my Holy Spirit adventures. If one of my children were lost, I would go to any lengths to bring them back. I understand the heart of God in sending me on these Holy Spirit Adventures through my love for you guys, though it pales in comparison to His own.

To my firstborn, Monica Bethany Lemke, thank you for giving me feedback and encouragement while being a source of wisdom and a sounding board for almost every chapter in this book. I know you have the gift of writing, and I am cheering you on as you PUBLISH! When I write, I think of you reading it and all the generations that will come after us.

The following pure souls took time away from their own lives to edit chapters in this book. A heartfelt thank you to each of you.

Dani Tucker
Emily Goudreault
Dana Navarrette
Clay and Antoinette Campbell
Monica Lemke
Morgan Webster
Joy Coker, my beautiful mom
Hollie Hutson
Lisa Watson
Jessica White
Emily Radler
Bryanna O'Keefe
Jonathon Weiss

PREFACE

I received a prophetic word, a message from God, many years before my adventures with the Holy Spirit began. A woman said that I was never meant to be in the four walls of the church. Another woman told me she saw me flying all over the globe and then doing a victory lap. These prophetic words seemed so strange at the time because I wasn't a big traveler then. All I wanted to do was find a place to serve within the church.

With prayer, I began to understand that God, of course, wanted me to be trained in the church, but my calling was outside the building we call church. I was to follow the Holy Spirit's leading to bring the good news of Jesus and to "seek and save" those who had lost their way. The church is changing, and it's a new season for the body of Christ. We have experienced a recent "dry bones" season. We are now becoming a rising army sent out to take territory and bring His kingdom.

God is doing a new thing that is an old strategy. Rather than gathering in the thousands, we are being sent out like the disciples to share the hopeful message we have in Jesus. We are both being led by the Spirit and, at the same time, being rooted and grounded in God's word.

"Now, about the gifts of the Spirit, brothers and sisters, I do not want you to be uninformed... **There are different kinds of gifts, but the same Spirit distributes them***. Now, to each one, the manifestation of the Spirit is given for the common good. To one, there is given through the Spirit a message of wisdom, to another a message of knowledge by means of the same Spirit, to another faith by the same Spirit, to another gifts of healing by that one Spirit, to another miraculous powers, to another prophecy, to another distinguishing between spirits, to another speaking in different kinds of tongues, and to still*

another the interpretation of tongues. All these are the work of one and the same Spirit, and he distributes them to each one, just as he determines."
1 Corinthians 12:1, 4-5, 7-11, NIV

Did these gifts end when the written word became available? My answer is this: Keep reading your Bible and ask the Holy Spirit. Watch and be alert for the way He answers you, and don't dismiss His answers as coincidence. He will speak to you through a sermon, a scripture, a song on the radio, or some other way. There are signs all around you if you will only ask the Holy Spirit to show you the way.

Let's do that now. If you are willing, say this prayer aloud:

Holy Spirit, open my eyes, ears, and heart to the things you want me to be aware of. Let all my spiritual, and even physical senses, be sensitive to you, God. I submit my will to the one true living God found in Jesus. Let your word be my anchor and foundation. I am not led by my mind, my own will, emotions or logic, but by Your Holy Spirit. Let your Spirit lead me into all truth. Amen.

"Ask, and it will be given to you; seek, and you will find; knock, and it will be opened to you. For everyone who asks receives, and he who seeks finds, and to him who knocks, it will be opened."
Matthew 7:7-8, ESV

"So we are messengers for Christ. God is using us to call people. So we are standing here for Christ and begging people, 'Come back to God!'"
2 Corinthians 5:20, WE version

The conversations I recount and quote within the following pages are to the best of my memory and not exact dialogue, as I didn't record myself or others. I journaled after the fact. This book is not meant to be a theological resource or replacement for the written word of God. The Bible is your handbook, your compass, and always your true north, so look to God's word for help and answers. Other resources I found helpful when learning to hear from God : Yahweh Speaks by Craig Cooney and Love Speaks-21 Ways to Recognize the Voice of God by Carl Wesley Anderson.

You can read this book through as you would a normal book, or treat it like a daily devotional for forty days which is my recommendation. Watch God prepare daily divine appointments as you read and pray through this book.

Happy Holy Spirit Adventures to you,

Jennifer

CHAPTER 1

WAITRESS IN THE SKY

I hadn't been a flight attendant long when I noticed God was sending me places to share the love and truth I have in my heart for Christ. I was on a layover in Tulsa, and my fellow FA (flight attendant) and I were debating whether to stay at the hotel or get out into the city. The "drawstring pants" were definitely calling my name since I had a 3:15 am wake-up call the next day. Fresh air won out over staring at the hotel room walls.

Our Uber driver, Connie, pulled up, and we hopped in. Somewhere during the short ride, she threw out the question, "What made you girls want to become flight attendants?"

My fellow flight attendant answered first. While she spoke, I thought about whether God wanted me to share my true story. I mean, those types of questions are just pleasantries for the most part. Maybe it's in the driver handbook to pretend to be interested, so you get that five-star rating?

I didn't have a traditional answer on the why. Travel the world? Nope, not without my family. The truth was I NEVER wanted to BE a flight attendant. I know that's hard for those who have always dreamed of doing it, but it was truly an act of obedience to God.

Two years before becoming a flight attendant, I was flying as a passenger with my hubby for an anniversary trip. The flight attendants on that flight were FUSSY. One flight attendant huffed and puffed when I dared ask for iced tea (I didn't know, but now I totally understand, it's a pain to make iced tea on an airplane!) I didn't hear God all the time during that season. I normally had impressions and thoughts that felt like my own, but sitting on that seat in the airplane, I heard God say so clearly, "You could change the atmosphere on an airplane."

I knew God changed the atmosphere of my life from one of chaos to peace, but I answered, "That's great, God, but I don't want to be a flight attendant. Be someone's waitress? Been there, done that." I know that's prideful. It became abundantly clear over the next year that is exactly where He wanted me to learn to serve with a pure heart and deal with that pride.

Back home, I tried to forget the words I'd heard on the airplane. However, when God speaks to me, and it's really Him, the message doesn't go away. It stays on repeat until I obey or silence it. Did you know we can silence the Holy Spirit? We can. It's like pressing snooze or stop on an alarm.

I remember one day when I was asking Him if he really wanted me to work as a flight attendant. I pulled a glass out of our pantry. My husband had brought it home from a golf tournament a few years before. I'd never noticed until that day that it had wings and an airline name embossed and etched into the glasses. I received many confirmations after that. Through signs and wonders, I knew that I was "called" to be a flight attendant and, in doing so, had unknowingly been drafted into my very own Holy Spirit adventure.

While being a flight attendant, I was able to allow His love to fill the airplane. When I poured a coke, they got a little taste of Him. When I sat on my jumpseat and prayed (I should say when I remembered to), His peace would invade. Even if I never said the name of Jesus, He was there...loving, touching, flowing through my hands. There were so many days that I wanted to strangle entitled passengers. I got frustrated with people who desperately sought control, but found out sometimes the weather doesn't obey their commands. There were also many days I had the honor of seeing His miracles and being an integral part of His plan. I would never have that honor of presenting Jesus if I'd chosen my comfort over obedience.

Sometimes when I share the real story about why I became a flight attendant, people give me an eyebrow raise, and I wonder if they're thinking, "You hear voices? Well, bless your heart." So I didn't really want to share with the driver, but I told my heavenly Father, "God, if you want me to share it, then she will ask me specifically."

Well, she asked. I shared and felt the happiness that comes after I put myself out there by God's leading. Connie, our driver, said that her pastor had started a new series at church. She and some ladies were meeting and discussing it. The subject was about hearing the voice of God. Connie said she desired to hear God but didn't know how.

My true story I shared with her was a testimony that carried power. If I could hear God, and God is no respecter of persons (Acts 10:34), then He could do it for her. I asked if I could pray for her, so she pulled over (Don't worry, she stopped the ride. I checked.) I then noticed the small cross dangling from her mirror. When she turned around to look at me, I saw her eyes. I can always tell in someone's eyes if they love Jesus. There's a kindness and a depth there. It was a sweet moment. My fellow flight attendant, who had grown up as a Christian but just wasn't "buying it" anymore, said she wanted to pray with us too. We prayed for Connie to hear the voice of God, and Connie prayed for protection over us on our travels.

THE MORAL OF THE STORY

I wanted the comfort of my hotel room, but I decided to follow the nudges of the Holy Spirit and have an adventure.

Your God stories are VALUABLE and life-changing. They carry power and don't ever "get old." Ask God to create an opportunity for you to share your testimony or encourage you through someone else's.

Then I heard the Lord asking, "Whom should I send as a messenger to this people? Who will go for us?" I said, "Here I am. Send me."
Isaiah 6:8, NIV

Question

Is God calling you to do something out of your comfort zone? Will you obey? Journal about it, including your hesitations and your fears, your hopes, and your dreams.

What do you need to follow Him and obey today?

Circle one:

Faith

Trust

Boldness

Courage

Strength

Or write your own word:

CHAPTER 2

POOPING ON THE PLANE

Holy Spirit adventures are often not about "getting in the salvation prayer." Many times these adventures are time spent learning lessons about who God is and how He works. I love this story, or lesson, and I remember it like it was yesterday. This guy, we'll call him Larry, boarded the plane with his doggy who we will call Percy because I didn't catch his name either, but he definitely had a "Percy" vibe with his little bow tie that doubled as his dog collar.

Larry is supposed to keep Percy in a kennel while on board because he's a pet on board and NOT a registered service or "medically necessary" animal. Larry pulled him out of the carrier and assured me, "'Percy is a veteran flier. He's flown overseas, and I've never had a problem. He always does great. Everyone says so, and they usually just let me keep him in my lap." Larry smiled and nodded his head as if willing me to do the same.

I give Percy, the pug, a little scratch. I let Larry know that while Percy may be an angel dog, he's required to remain in his carrier for our 2-hour flight. I like dogs better than people, but we couldn't very well put Larry in the kennel, could we?

So when I see Larry barreling down the aisle towards me carrying Percy, I am perplexed. Dude, we've had this conversation. But then I noticed a...errr... substance running down from Percy onto Larry's light tan pants. Aw, man.

INCOMING!

And I'm ready for them. I push the lavatory door open. Larry apparently thought Percy would finish his business on the toilet, so he hovered the pup over the open seat. Percy pawed the air. In 'hindsight' (pun intended), I'm sure Larry later realized this was a bad idea.

Larry held Percy over the right spot for a bit, but Percy said, "No go, Larry."

Larry tried to hand Percy to me. I backed up. NOPE! This is your deal. So he put Percy down and jerked on the paper towels letting them flutter around the tiny lav and onto the floor. He wet some of the paper towels in a desperate but futile attempt to erase Percy's mess from his pants. Now on the carpet in the aisle, Percy immediately let it all out on his preferred potty spot. The smell was PUNGENT. In training, we had been trained on toxic fume events, but nothing could have prepared me for this.

Percy, though a "veteran flier," was not having a good day on the plane.

I was so tempted to blame this on Larry. Maybe Percy doesn't do well left behind in a kennel, but it was Percy who did the deed. I had played the role of "the mean, old flight attendant" who made Percy get in his little kennel when other flight attendants let him ride in Larry's lap. That probably stressed him out. Percy was the victim here. He did nothing wrong but have a nervous stomach. This situation was forced upon him. Believe me. I saw his big pug eyes. He would rather have been ANYWHERE ELSE than on that plane pooping on his owner's pants.

Whose fault was it?

God even uses comical situations to speak truth to me. I saw that, like Percy, we can be put in situations we should NOT be in.

How many times have we seen this play out? A father leaves his little boy. Little boy grows up healthy on the outside but has a handicapped heart. Who is going to step up and teach him how to be a man now?

Or, maybe, dad stays but unleashes all his anger and frustration onto his children.

The cancer diagnosis.

The miscarriage.

The job layoff.

The picture posted by another we never intended to share with the world.

We play hot potato with shame and blame.

I saw it time and time again on the airplane, and I have learned that none of us get out of this world unharmed or untouched by the enemy. We are the walking "pooped" on. We live in a world full of blame, and it is CRAZY MAKING. Blame them. Blame ourselves. Blame God because isn't He ultimately in charge? Blame the airline. Blame the passenger. Blame the government. Blame the people who kneel, or don't kneel, or don't agree with us. People who struggle with perfection and insecurity look for someone to blame. I know I've done it. Don't go down that road. It's a dead end. We aren't warring with flesh and blood. (Ephesians 6:12) That's really how we can walk victoriously through this life. Not pointing fingers, demanding perfection, or finding fault. We can be honest, adjust and move forward with God's wisdom when someone is unsafe, or the situation isn't working.

Now, back to our bathroom fail on the plane. The deed had been done. There was no use crying over spilled poo. Larry was practically in tears. He was on his hands and knees attempting to clean up Percy's mess. He was smearing it in a circle while robotically repeating the same phrases over and over, "I'm so sorry. I'm so sorry. Percy never does this. He's normally such a good dog. I can't believe it."

I could tell Larry was trying to do his part, and my heart softened.

I said, "Leave it, Larry. I'll finish this. Take care of Percy and then get him back in the kennel."

I said this because Larry was actually making an even bigger mess with his frantic scrubbing.

MORAL OF THE STORY

To be able to have our own Holy Spirit adventures, we have to ask God to silence the accuser's voice in our head and have an understanding that blame leads nowhere. Judgment will block the love from flowing out of our hearts. We might be a victim, but we don't have to stay there. A mess is a mess. It has to be cleaned up so we can move on.

And now, dear brothers and sisters, one final thing. Fix your thoughts on what is true, honorable, right, pure, lovely, and admirable. Think about things that are excellent and worthy of praise.
Philippians 4:8, NLT

Question

Do you struggle with wanting to find fault? Ask God to show you
if you do and journal about it. The process of writing it out will
allow you to put your thoughts on paper and wait for an answer
from the Holy Spirit. You can then hear clearly and discern
situations as they truly are and give empathy a chance to grow.
What do you need from God today to keep your eyes fixed on him?

Circle one:

Faith

Hope

A revelation of His love

Grace

Purity

Or an emotional support animal ;)

Or write your own

CHAPTER 3

CALLED TO PEOPLE

I was about to slide into an empty booth in the bustling food court at the Chicago airport when this guy pushed past me and took my spot. I looked at him sideways with eyebrows raised.

The only other open seat was at a community table. It was the Christmas season. After two flights down for the day, and one more to go, I was "peopled out." I wanted some space. The airplane is basically one giant community table in the sky. I looked around, but I had no other choice.

I would have one open seat on either side of me for the time being. I studied the kid across the table from my proposed seat. Would he be a "talker?" You learn to sum people up in about 2 seconds on the airplane. He looked like my youngest son and aloof to the world around. Not the talker type. Good to go.

I took my seat across from him and made sure to keep my headphones in. I made a mental note of the gold bling on his neck. The chain was heavy, but the cross that hung on it was delicate. The interesting jewelry spilled out over his sweater and even his parka. Either he was a rapper, or he loved Jesus.

Was this a divine appointment?

I asked the Lord, "How do you see this young man?"

The words flooded my mind:

- Frontiersman
- John Wayne

- Lead the way
- Independent
- Doesn't need a lot of anything or anyone
- Lonely

Sigh. I guess God wanted me to "people" again today.

That's the thing with following the Holy Spirit, there are so many lonely, hurting people who need God's love. The world is like an overcrowded emergency room with too few people willing to learn the lessons of love. We don't know how to love, and we don't want to follow the Holy Spirit to bring His healing touch.

Bleh. I pulled the earphones out.

Should I say something? Everyone within earshot got up and left. The Holy Spirit had evacuated the area. I felt a God nod!

I started with something we might have in common.

"That's a nice necklace."

As the conversation progressed, I learned that the young man was:

A student from Czechoslovakia traveling home

Despite the necklace, not a Jesus lover

He was not, in fact, a rapper

The necklace was a gift from his great grandmother to her grandchildren before she passed away at the ripe old age of ninety. His father had pulled a re-gift and given the cross pendant to him.

The young man then told a fascinating story about the original gift giver. His great grandmother lived through the Holocaust! She was German, but she married a Czechoslovakian soldier who would be his great grandfather. She was punished for betraying her country by marrying a soldier of the enemy, so the Nazis arrested her. His great grandmother was sent to a concentration camp called Theresienstadt. Miraculously, she lived through it and had the tattooed numbers on her arm to prove her imprisonment. Her husband lived too and this is how the necklace was passed down through the generations.

I said, "So, she was a Christian? Your great grandmother, I mean."

He responded with his accent, "Maybe. I don't know. Maybe she was Catholic or something."

"Well, do you think that's why she gave your dad the cross... Because she loved Jesus?"

He stuttered, "How do I say this? Religion in Europe is not like the United States. People in Europe don't really believe in God anymore."

He was basically saying he didn't believe in God.

I could have put a placid look on my face, "Hmm that's interesting," dropped the subject, and started eating my now cold food.

The Holy Spirit respects people's boundaries. It is hard to explain, but I have an inner knowing when I have completed an assignment from God. If I have that peace, I can confidently end the conversation. I've done my part to plant a seed. God will continue to water it.

I knew in my heart of hearts this assignment was not finished. Something came over me in that moment. I was filled with a Holy Spirit boldness. I knew I had to forge ahead. I felt a sense of urgency. I was fueled by knowing this young man may not ever have another moment like this in his life since he was headed back to Europe.

I envisioned his great grandmother watching on from Heaven begging, "Please DON'T STOP, God. PLEASE! Do not let him leave that table. That's my legacy!" As a mother and grandmother, I would want the Holy Spirit to keep pushing the witness to give my future generations a chance to know Jesus. No matter how far they had wandered from the path of truth, I would be begging God to give them one more chance. I would not, could not, squander this moment. Great grandma was watching!

I didn't beat around the bush. I said, "Well, sometimes, God sends me to people whose relatives have gone on to Heaven, and they want their family to know that God is real. Their generations want them to be in Heaven with them one day. I felt like I heard something for you about how God sees you. Would it be okay if I shared that?"

The blonde-headed boy's eyes opened big, and then there was an awkward pause. "Um. Okay."

I would have respected his no, but I would have really loved an enthusiastic, "YES! PLEASE!"

I shared the John Wayne/frontiersman/lead-the-way stuff. Maybe it's wishful thinking, but he seemed to relate and soak it in like a cool drink of water.

I continued, "God is real. I think your great grandmother would want you to know that. God brought her through the Holocaust, or you wouldn't be here sitting with me. The Bible says we are surrounded by a great cloud of witnesses. She is watching right now!"

He said, "I don't know. I don't know if God is real."

He didn't sound jaded or hardened. He sounded like he was searching.

I said, "Well, thank you for being honest with me. I'm not trying to push anything on you, but God is real. The proof is hanging right around your neck. You chose to wear it today. My job sent me to this place today, hundreds of miles from my home, and here I am, talking to you. It's not a coincidence." He looked thoughtful.

I said, "Hey, I don't even know your name. I'm Jennifer."

The young man said, "My name is Jacob or Yakov in my country."

We shook hands.

I said, "Are you named after the Jacob in the Bible?"

Jacob asked, "This is how little I know about God. I had no idea my name was in the Bible."

I told him the story of Jacob being a twin, the younger brother, but being the leader. God chose the second born to lead. I'm not sure what this meant to him, but he was nodding his head and listening. Maybe he was a twin? I don't know. The story of Jacob reminded me of the word from God that this young man was to "lead the way."

I felt a release. I had completed my assignment from God. Now it was up to God to do what only He could do. Truth was spoken. Love was delivered. The seed had been planted. Jacob would decide to open his heart or not.

I scooted my chair back. "It's been a pleasure to talk with you, but I have to go now, Jacob. Remember this, either I'm just some crazy religious lady you met at an airport, or I'm bringing you a really important message. Keep your eyes open. If they are showing a John Wayne picture on the airplane or if you see some other confirmation of what I said, or even if you already feel it in your heart, then you need to consider that God is real, and He is talking to you."

I headed to my next flight to end the twelve-hour day. As I walked, I talked to God. Instead of feeling drained, I now felt energized. I wasn't sure how all that went, but I asked God to please confirm things for Jacob, cover my mistakes, let Jacob hear what he needed to hear, and send more people to talk to him about Jesus. (As you are reading, will you agree with me in that prayer?)

I smiled as I walked and put my headphones in. A song by Mark Schultz came on. I hadn't heard the song in ages. The lyrics are about someone who has gone on to Heaven and wants to be remembered still. "I remember you. Will you remember me? Remember me in a Bible cracked and faded... child of wonder, child of God. I remember you. Will you remember me?" These words sang out into my ears. I felt the pleasure of God over me and his love for Jacob, and tears streamed down my face.

THE MORAL OF THE STORY

If we don't deliver the messages of love and truth, who will?

We might be too tired. Tired of "people-ing." We might not get the response that makes us feel warm and fuzzy, but God calls us to His people. We won't be perfect in our delivery. We may fumble, but God will cover us if we keep a humble heart. The words you deliver from the heart of God to His beloved could be the difference between life and death, between heaven and hell. Obedience energizes us with God's power. Will you say yes to God? Be on the lookout for opportunities and be bold and brave!

"Therefore, since we are surrounded by such a great cloud of witnesses, let us throw off everything that hinders and the sin that so easily entangles. And let us run with perseverance the race marked out for us, fixing our eyes on Jesus, the pioneer and perfecter of faith. For the joy set before him, he endured the cross, scorning its shame, and sat down at the right hand of the throne of God. Consider him who endured such opposition from sinners so that you will not grow weary and lose heart."
Hebrews 12:1-3, NIV

Read Luke 16:19-31 for an interesting truth. People who are no longer on earth want their future generations to know the truth of Heaven and Hell and to be offered an opportunity to repent. Repentance can't come through someone who is dead but, instead, through God's words and His prophets.

Question

What do you need to "people" today?

Circle one:

Bravery

Fresh love

The gift of prophecy

Ears to hear God's voice

The fruits of the Holy Spirit

Or write your own

....

CHAPTER 4

NO NORMAL WITH THE HOLY SPIRIT

It was Christmas Day, doing a short turn to Tampa. What could go wrong?

What I'm learning is there is rarely a "normal" flight. There's always something going down on the plane. Everyone's personal boundaries are crushed. Babies get hungry and cry. It's what they do. People have tummy issues from turbulence or rough landings or nerves. Remember Percy, the pug? Schtuff happens. People annoy each other. Yeah, that actually happens a lot.

Sometimes, I "got people problems" on the plane because people get crazy when you have 150-200 of them shoved in a metal tube. It can get ugly. Really quick.

Today would be different, though. Why? Because it was CHRISTMAS! Everyone would be kind to each other. We would share joy and peace on earth and on the airplane! God bless ye, merry gentlemen! I had an arsenal of cheer, a smile, a light-up reindeer antler headband, and a stocking full of coloring books with chocolates.

I was working first-class that day, and the gate agent informed me there would be two dogs up front, one a service animal and one a medically necessary dog. I love doggies, as you know, so I told her, "No problem...as long as they are well behaved." I thought of Percy again, and as long as they can "hold it."

I began doing my service and handing out hot towels. A woman in the last

row of first-class beckons me to come closer. "Can I help you?" She motions me
closer. "Yes?" I'm bending down to hear because now we are whispering, so I
know she will likely be tattling. Happens all the time.

"There are TWO dogs up here, and I am HIGHLY allergic. One is within four
feet of me." She tilted her head and held one hand up to shield the other as
she pointed to the couple across the aisle. A little mini wienie dog was wrapped
up in its owner's arms like a little Christmas gift. His brown eyes peered back
innocently, "Who me?"

Allergy-lady continued, "This happened on another airline, even when I told
them right away. THEY had the nerve to remove ME and not the DOG from an
airplane." She mopped her face nervously with the hot towel.

I shared with allergy-lady, "My husband and I were just having this conversation
last night. How do we prioritize one need versus the harm done to another. It's a real
problem, and I'm sorry. Can I bring you anything to help, or do you have Benadryl?"

"No, no. I just don't think it's fair, and I wanted you to know."

"I completely understand. Please let me know if I can do anything for you."
She nodded, and we stopped whispering.

Later, as I delivered drinks, I noticed the wienie dog lady handed her pup to
her husband on the aisle closer to the allergy lady.

I discreetly went to her and said gently, "I love your puppy. He's so adorable
and sweet. The lady across the aisle happens to be highly allergic to dogs, so if you
could keep him near the window, that might help her?"

"Well, of course!" Wienie dog woman said quickly. She snatched the dog back
from her husband on the aisle. A few minutes later, I hear from her direction,
"Psssssst!"

Wienie dog woman wanted me to lean in closer as the other woman had. I
sensed another tattle coming on.

She hissed, "She was pointing at me earlier, and I knew it! Do you know that
no one is actually "allergic" to dogs. It's their fur, and we have a short-haired dog.
There's virtually NO chance of her having a reaction unless I rub his body on her
face." She continued whispering heatedly, getting closer to my face, "My dog is
medically necessary for my seizures, and SHE is complaining about ME when she
brought all those ridiculous bags as carry-ons!"

I said, "I understand it's not an ideal situation for anyone. I happen to love
your sweet puppy, and he happens to be my favorite passenger on board." She
smiled and softened.

Despite the whispers, everybody can hear everything on the airplane if they
are paying attention. The two women then had a vicious staring contest. As they

went to the lavs, there were lots of huffs and side eyes to indicate their mutual indignance at the situation. For the most part, I sensed they both felt heard and understood though. God's peace de-escalated a potentially ugly situation. Three things to know when following the Holy Spirit:

1. **Learning to love people who can't or won't act right is part of our time here on this earth.**
   When we operate in love, honor means not taking sides and assigning a bad guy and a victim.
   Question & heart check: Is our love genuine and our concern real? Do we have empathy and compassion for other people's pain? People sniff out a fake in two seconds. In short, they know if we care by the warmth or coldness in our response.

2. **Know what you carry within you from God.**
   Remember, God told me I could be an atmosphere changer with him. What do you carry from your heavenly Father's heart to earth?

3. **Everyone wants to be loved and comforted in their struggles.**
   There is a fine line between people-pleasing and love. People-pleasing means we are trying to manage someone else's emotions. I find that's when situations actually spiral out of control. People don't like to be "managed." I have learned to listen, validate and hear hearts to be a peacemaker instead of controlling, managing, or trying to intimidate people into compliance. We can be peace-makers instead of peace-keepers.

Take away: People are CRAZY. Just kidding.

I've learned on the plane, when I get people sometimes at their worst, to focus on love and care, and that solves 99% of "people problems." It's kind of simple. We all just want to be loved and accepted. We need the Holy Spirit to have wisdom and discernment and to show love to everyone involved. Many days I'm worn out and empty. There is no peace or loving flowing from my empty cup. I don't always feel God's love in my heart. I have to take a moment and ask God how He sees the people in front of me. Then the love can flow.

"May the Lord make your love increase and overflow for each other and for everyone else, just as ours does for you."
1 Thessalonians 3:12, NIV

Question

Do you ever feel yourself getting triggered? Do you feel the fight, flight, or freeze responses kicking in? If we ask, the Holy Spirit can guide us through the emotions we feel and navigate around the emotional overflow of others. Journal about any emotions (yours or anothers) you are feeling overwhelmed with today.

Circle one:

Jesus

Love

Joy

Being built on God's foundation

Burdens lifted

Or write your own

....

CHAPTER 5

STANDBY WITH THE HOLY SPIRIT

The clock showed I was 30 minutes shy of finishing up my standby time at DFW. My phone blurted out the special, and quite annoying, ring of Crew Scheduling. "Flight attendant Weiss, we have a trip for you."

Bed wouldn't come until about 3:00 AM. I wanted to cry, but I remembered, this time, to encourage myself in the Lord. It wasn't a bad trip. One leg to Jacksonville and then one back the following evening. I didn't even have to work the leg back. I could sit in a passenger seat and read my book. The next day was my husband's birthday. I called Crew Scheduling with a very standard request, "Can I get an earlier flight back since I'm not working the flight?" In a very clipped response, she said, "No, we aren't releasing anyone right now." Bummer.

I decided to make the most of it. My husband's grandfather owned a radio shop many moons ago in downtown Jacksonville, so I set off trying to find it the following day. I found the old storefront of his shop and said a prayer honoring the generations before us that had walked these very streets.

I popped in a coffee shop across the road. A fully tatted girl took my order. Everything but her very pretty face was covered with tattoo flair. I'll call her Amy since she looked a lot like Amy Winehouse. I thought about asking her if I could make a tattoo interpretation with the help of the Holy Spirit.

What, you might ask, is a tattoo interpretation? It's really easy. I ask the Holy Spirit to tell me the meaning behind their tattoos. I love doing this and meeting people where they are. Many have an idea about the spiritual realm, but some haven't met anyone who would tell them about the Holy Spirit. God wants to reveal his heart to his children. There is a reason they chose that specific tattoo and why they are drawn to the words or images.

I thought about asking if she was interested in an interpretation, but it was busy in the tiny little shop. The music blared as I tried to shout my order. The singer crooned, "Don't go down to the water's edge. I didn't do it, but I saw who did. This ain't no f-ing game..."

Yeah, I decided it wasn't a good time to make a tattoo interpretation. I felt like I was in the enemy's territory. Did I have authority here? I asked God. If I was to speak, the Holy Spirit would create an opportunity.

A friend of mine hand made prophetic artwork for an event. I had extras, and I had stuffed them in the side pocket of my bag "just in case."

I took one out and looked at it. The hand-drawn flowers were so beautiful, and it included a scripture of encouragement. I asked God what He wanted me to write on the blank back side of the paper. I wrote out what I felt He was saying and gave it to Amy.

Later, she smiled and waved from across the room but didn't come chat. I thought my divine delivery trip was over. I could put a big checkmark by the Holy Spirit adventure on this trip, but there was more to come.

I went to a cool restaurant inside a museum. My waitress happened to be named Faith. I knew she was named by God. I pulled out another one of my emergency prophetic pieces of art with scripture and left it for her on the table with a nice tip.

Later, I felt like God shared something with me. Both of these women, Faith and tattoo girl, were or would soon be pregnant, and they would be considering terminating their pregnancies and the little lives within. I remembered the writing on the prophetic artwork to Faith, "THE HOPE INSIDE YOU. Don't worry about anything. God's got this." The word I felt led to write confirmed this revelation. Hope was INSIDE her. I prayed that she would keep her baby and name her Hope!

I walked down the street and thanked God for sending me to this city. Even though I couldn't be with my husband on his birthday, I was grateful. I asked God for another confirmation that this was, in fact, about little babies. Was God wooing these women with these simple but beautiful notes with His words from scripture written on them? Was he giving their babies a voice through these words?

He confirmed it in my heart by the following:

He brought back to memory that an Amber Alert went off while I was in the restaurant with Faith. Everyone's phones started emitting their emergency tone. There was a lost child in the Jacksonville area. Yes, these babies were sending out a distress signal. Help me!

The day of my standby, I had stopped in at a coffee shop on my way to the airport. I had written a prophetic word for the barista. I started the word in bold print MOTHER'S HEART and victory. I gave it to her, and she readily received it and introduced herself. She shared her name was Laura and it meant victory.

I looked, with eyes wide, at the signpost on the INTERSECTING CORNER of BOTH the tattooed girl's business and the restaurant where Faith worked. The street was named Laura. Not only that, but these waist-high pillars said "Laura" as street markers. I'd never seen street signs like these on all my travels.

It was a sign from God that these women indeed had mothers' hearts and that there was victory here. Maybe they felt lost or alone or were afraid to have a baby? I don't know. You might think that I'm trying to connect things that don't connect. I've been walking long enough with the Holy Spirit to recognize that He is bringing me confirmations and not coincidences. He encourages us along our journey with these simple signs if we have eyes to see.

I pray Faith and tat girl let their babies live. Whether they decide to have their children or not, God loves and cherishes them and will hear them any time they call. Having two abortions, I do not understand why God allows me to deliver messages like these. His grace through the sacrifice and resurrection of Jesus is so beautiful. I do have two babies in heaven who are likely praying for me to save as many as I can, despite my own mistakes.

THINGS TO REMEMBER WHEN FOLLOWING THE HOLY SPIRIT AND DELIVERING MESSAGES

1. **Authority.**
   I thought it was interesting that my husband's grandfather had lived in this town for decades and had been a business owner. I had authority there with that connection. I had an "eviction notice" from Heaven for the enemy if he tried to stop me from delivering these words that God wanted delivered. Jesus went to Hell and he holds the keys to freedom.

2.   **Offense.**
    If I get offended while on a Holy Spirit assignment or distracted from
    my mission by cuss words, crazy music, tattoos of devils, or thrown off
    by appearance, then I won't do much good for God's kingdom. He is
    sending us to the lost ones.

I'm in the editing phase of this book and listening to some music. I was reading it
and, even with all the confirmations above, I started to hear the accuser say, "You
are making all this up." I struggled with even including this particular story for
some reason. But the lyrics sang out, and I heard them in my heart, "I'm standing
under the waterfall of your approval, and I find that I don't need anything else
or anyone else but you. You call me your own. A child you chose before I took a
breath." I know that God wants this in, and I know the enemy wants it out.

"And I will ask the Father, and he will give you another Comforter, Counselor, Helper,
Intercessor, Advocate, Strengthener, and Standby, that he may remain with you forever."
John 14:16, AMP

Go easy on those who hesitate in the faith. Go after those who take the wrong way. Be
tender with sinners, but not soft on sin. The sin itself stinks to high heaven. Another version
says, "...You can snatch burning sticks out of the fire..."
Jude 1:22-23, MSG

Question

How can I walk in the authority of the Lord?

Circle one:

Love

God glasses

The power of Jesus

A Scripture from God's word to stand on

Or write your own

....

CHAPTER 6

I'M OKAY

I was In Kihei, Maui trying to find a breakfast place on Yelp. I was lost as per usual. I walked through a narrow walkway through buildings to see if the restaurant was around the corner. I peeked around, and there stood a young woman with booty shorts and a short crop top that showed her stretch-marked tummy talking on her phone. She hung up and took a seat on the bench. Putting her hands over her face, she started crying quietly. My heart hurt for her. I walked over and put my hand on her shoulder, "Are you okay, sweet girl?" She didn't look up but cried harder and said, "I'm okay. Really. I'll be okay."

I said, "I'm so sorry you are hurting."

She said, "No, it's okay."

I kind of figured it wasn't okay. She didn't look like the praying kind, but I've been wrong about that. I gently said, "Can I pray for you?"

"It's really nothing." I gathered she wasn't comfortable with praying.

She stood up and wiped her eyes. "I'm okay."

How many times had she said that?

Sensing God set this opportunity up, I asked her, "May I give you a hug?"

She sniffed and nodded bravely. She was still trying to convince herself, and me, that she was okay.

We embraced, and she lost it again. I was able to whisper through her cries, "God's mercies are new every day for you. God loves you so much." I just repeated that. I held her for what felt like a full minute.

"Thank you. I'm okay, really."

I prayed for her as she walked away, "Let her see you clearly, God. Be so real to her today, God. Love her like she's never been loved. You are the only one who can love her as she deserves to be loved."

What I learned on that Holy Spirit-led adventure:

DIRECTION

I got lost, but I now see how God used my navigational mistakes as stalling and leading me to that tiny alcove between buildings at the exact moment she needed a hug. It breaks a Father's heart when we cry and are hurting. He knows when we are not okay.

He sends his messengers to comfort the hurting with His love.

Our arms are His arms.

Hugs are simple. They heal.

"The LORD appeared to us in the past, saying: "I have loved you with an everlasting love; therefore, I have drawn you with unfailing kindness."
Jeremiah 31:3, NIV

Question

If you make a wrong turn, encounter traffic, or a roadblock, do you get frustrated? You can ask God to rewire your brain to see setbacks as setups for divine appointments. Journal about your frustrations and give them to God.

What do you need to be able to be the hands, arms, and feet of Jesus?

Circle one:

Peace

Obedience

Boldness

Direction

Softened heart

Or write your own

CHAPTER 7

NOT SO PRETTY DAYS

While I experienced miraculous days when I was intentional about letting the Holy Spirit lead me, I also had long days with mechanical problems when I worked through the days glumly missing my family. I experienced confusing days where I followed the Holy Spirit, but things didn't work the way I thought they would. I want to be authentic about the not so pretty days. The Holy Spirit is training us in faith. While adventures with the Holy Spirit are so much fun, we are also learning to persevere and be steadfast. True faith is when you still believe even when you can't see. Oh, how I love the days that everything falls in line, though.

A great day for me:

The parking spot is front and center when I get to the airport.

I remember to bring my lunch, work ID, and the right clothes.

I get an email from my supervisor that someone reported me for being AWESOME.

Things click, and the divine appointments flow. People are receptive to what I share, and I see God work miracles.

I go through these days firing on all cylinders, and I am physically and spiritually flying. On these days, I JUST KNOW that God is with me.

On the "not so pretty days":

I wake up with a headache.

I have to get up at 3 AM.

I feel overwhelmed by all the needy people.

A customer is rude or difficult, and I hate my job.

I am delayed by traffic and almost late for sign-in.

The crew is too different than me for my taste, or they are mean.

The world is unkind to me.

On these days, I have thoughts like, "Why am I even doing this? It's pointless."

Do you ever have days like this even when all you want to do is love people and love Jesus, but the world just won't cooperate?

When I have cruddy days, I start looking for a reason.

Bad days mean I am not blessed and have lost my way.

God has forgotten me.

He has something more important to do than help me.

He loves someone else more and is blessing them with a good day because they are good or perfect or whatever.

I try to encourage myself in the Lord, but I find it hard to be joyful on days like these. How could I? I'm doing a job that is not my first choice or even on my list of things I want to do.

I tend to shut my heart down on days like this. Just me. Alone. Against the world. Trying to help people who don't want to be helped.

It hurts too much to stay open, honest, loving, kind, and step out in faith again. After I shut down, the enemy swoops in with shame and lies. I blame myself. I need to do better. Try harder. Or I blame other people. The dumb wreck that made me late. The customers who take, take, take but don't give.

"Yes, it's their fault!"

They need to change. If things would JUST BE DIFFERENT, then I could too, and I would be happy and could share this blasted good news I carry!

I've learned it, and it was a hard lesson to learn. I CANNOT let my circumstances dictate my JOY and PEACE found only in God!

I've struggled since I was called to this job. I know I am being obedient to the Holy Spirit, serving cokes and picking up trash on an airplane. I've never wanted to do it. I was honestly terrible at it when I first started. It's an easy job, but I couldn't get the order of things straight, and the people who were there that WANTED to be there caught on really easily. Yet, here I was struggling and unhappy.

Some days, I could see the beauty in it.

There ARE Holy Spirit-led adventures.

God sends me on divine appointments, and I see miracles. However, my dislike and unhappiness for the actual job, dealing with difficult people and uncontrollable circumstances started poisoning my mind. A passenger was extremely dreadful, calling me a very nasty name, and it just made me want to avoid going to work. Ever. Again. I was in a rough season. I was becoming blinded and unaware of God moments and opportunities. I could no longer see the miracles. I cried out to God many times in despair during this time.

I had done all I knew to do to find joy. I prayed, searched the bible and decreed his word. I asked God for help with my attitude, I worshipped, and I spent more dedicated time with Him. I was desperate. But I'd been battling some pretty big giants lately on the airplane, and I was ready to tap out.

Every time I prayed and asked God if I could quit, I heard a gentle whisper, "Keep going."

And I also knew in my spirit that all this resistance was real, but it was just a test.

A friend sent me this scripture when I was at one of my lowest points.

"Serve wholeheartedly, as if you were serving the Lord, not people."
Ephesians 6:7 NIV

I persevered but I know it was God who gave me the strength to do so. In spite of all, I know the truth. God loves me and is always, always a good Father. The Holy Spirit is still with me, even, and especially, on hard days. I don't need to change my situation to fix my unhappiness. I'm right where God wants me to be. Resistance means I am chosen to carry something and Someone very special. My flesh is so weak but God's spirit in me is strong. My maturity must be fully grown. I'm not working for kudos or even for people. My character MUST BE refined until it is the purest of silver and gold.

"Consider it PURE joy brethren and ("sistren") when you encounter various trials of MANY kinds because you know that the TESTING of your faith produces perseverance. LET PERSEVERANCE finish its work so that you may be mature and complete, not lacking anything."
James 1:2-4, NIV

"...we also glory in our sufferings, because we know that suffering produces perseverance; perseverance, character; and character, hope. And hope does not put us to shame, because God's love has been poured out into our hearts through the Holy Spirit, who has been given to us."
Romans 5:3-5 NIV

Question

Do you ever get down on days when things aren't going your way? Ask the Holy Spirit to give you His perspective and share what this day is about by journaling through it.

What do you need to find joy in the Holy Spirit?

Circle one:

Peace

Fearlessness

A tender heart

Joy

A heavenly mindset

Or write your own

....

CHAPTER 8

DIVINE APPOINTMENTS

I was eating breakfast at a local restaurant, and I felt like I had a word from my heavenly Father for a lady. I heard some jumbled stuff, but what finally formed in my brain was "how to," and "with hope." I also heard the word "house." I was a little nervous to deliver the message because, well, what if it confused her? I certainly didn't understand it. I asked God to create an opportunity. If he did so, that would be my cue to share what I'd heard with her, even if it was disjointed. I went to grab a lid for my drink, and she was standing right beside them. This was my confirmation. I asked her if I could share something with her that I felt I'd heard from God. She said, stone-faced, "I'm listening."

That was my "go" signal. She had given me permission.

I learned that her name was Regina. I told her I wasn't crystal clear on it, but I'd heard from the Lord "how to" and "with hope" and something about a house.

Regina responded that she had a non-profit for homeless people. She, herself, had been homeless for two years.

"I've been trying for a while," she'd said, "to create a system where others would "house" the homeless. I've already been feeding them. It would be clean. Do background checks. Let people know what they were getting into, and then, if willing, they would offer an extra room in their home to someone without a home for ninety days to get back on their feet."

Her website is www.OTHfeedsthehungry.wordpress.com

The OTH in the link stands for on the HOUSE!

Isn't the Holy Spirit cool? I just love being set up by God on these divine appointments and walking them out in faith even when I don't fully understand.

"For when you saw me hungry, you fed me. When you found me thirsty, you gave me something to drink. When I had no place to stay, you invited me in, and when I was poorly clothed, you covered me. When I was sick, you tenderly cared for me, and when I was in prison, you visited me.'"
Matthew 25:35-36, TPT

Question

What's keeping you from going on your own Holy Spirit adventure today? Journal about it and then tell God you will be obedient. Listen for the nudges and follow them!

What do you need to change your perspective from an earthly one to a heavenly one?

Circle one:

Boldness

Courage

Gift of prophecy

An obedient heart

Directions from God

Or write your own

....

CHAPTER 9

SHARING

I was on a layover in Austin, Texas, and visiting one of my fav restaurants. I wanted to order one of everything on the menu! Holy Spirit adventures are fun in more ways than one!

I asked the waiter if I could order a single biscuit and a single donut instead of the full portions.

"Sure, no problem," the waiter chimed.

The hostess seated a group of four girls right next to me. We shared a couch/bench. It was a little awkward, and it felt a bit like being squished in the same booth with strangers.

These lovelies were pretty, chatty, twenty to thirty-year-old, stylish girls doing a Saturday girls' brunch. I was feeling a little lonely hearing the light hearted laughter that comes from connection. It was a challenge being away from my family on the weekend, but I was trying to enjoy myself and connect with God instead.

I put my headphones in, but the ladies were so close I could still hear every word. I couldn't help but listen to their conversation about Donald Trump (umm, not DT fans) and relationship stuff. Things were said like, "Are you going to hook up with... this guy is so hot...so and so got into management cuz she..." These girls were straight outta the Sex in the City show.

My waiter came up and helped me with my anti-eavesdropping efforts. Good news/bad news. Good news: Yes to a single biscuit. Bad news: The chef said no to a single donut hole. I was devastated. *puts hand to head*

"If I must, I must. Give me all five donut holes."

I prayed and gave thanks for my meal. I ate my most delicious warm flaky biscuit with orange marmalade jelly, and then I moved on to my first donut hole. YUM!

I contemplated my situation. Four donut holes left... only one of me. I still had two more courses to go. My stomach might possibly explode.

I had heard my brunching neighbors ordering. They debated over whether the brunch appetizers would feed them all. There were four donuts left and four of them.

I leaned over towards them, "Would you ladies like these? I'm not going to be able to finish them."

One of the girls responded, "No, thank you." One of the others said, "I'm not going to turn down a donut hole!"

She was my kind of girl.

I said, "I've never met a donut hole I didn't like."

"Me neither!" she laughed. I'd met a fellow foodie.

I slid them over. "God bless you," I said.

Normally, I wouldn't say that, but it rolled off my tongue, and I knew it was from God. They smiled. I was a wee bit surprised that they didn't push the donuts back my way.

My waiter brought my check, "I am sorry we couldn't do the single, so I took the donut holes off your check."

The ladies wrapped up their lunch and, as they stood to leave, the donut-loving girl said, "Thank you for sharing with us," and the other 3 echoed with a "Yeah, thanks." Even the "no" girl had ended up eating one.

I know how intentional God is with divine appointments... maybe I shared more than just donuts? Maybe I shared a deep knowing within my own heart with the "God bless you." Pre-Jesus, I ran the bars and looked for love in all the wrong places. I was never satisfied. I put on a tough front pretending that I wasn't empty. Deep down inside, I felt all alone. I lived my life like everything was up to me. I prayed they would receive God's love and peace in their hearts.

A song came on in my earphones as I walked away from the restaurant, "... Everyone needs compassion. Everyone needs the kindness of a savior... so take me as you find me all my fears and failures..." The next song that cycled up said, "I've never known love like this before..."

As I've shared, God talks to me through songs on my adventures. The Holy Spirit was leading me to love them right where they were . I was sent to plant the seed of blessing by giving to them. I decided that too close for comfort brunch was a God set up. The sweet little warm donut holes were a gift from the lover of their soul. The chef splitting the biscuits but not the donut holes? Odd or God? Again, call me crazy, but I know that it was orchestrated by God.

When we start to judge or think that others aren't open to His blessing, remember that only God knows the personal pain and emptiness we each carry. God is sending us to find the lost sheep. We don't have to convert them. That's not our job! Only the Holy Spirit moving on their heart can do that.

A spiritual concept to remember when following the Holy Spirit: When they accepted the donuts and took them into their bodies, they chose to taste and see how good God really is to them. He is our bread. Life is sweeter with Him, wouldn't you agree?

"Refuse to be a critic full of bias toward others, and you will not be judged. For you'll be judged by the same standard that you've used to judge others. The measurement you use on them will be used on you. Why would you focus on the flaw in someone else's life and fail to notice the glaring flaws of your own?"
Matthew 7:1-3, TPT

Question

Are you intimidated by the things others say or the way they look or act? Ask God to give you "God glasses." When I think about my own missteps, it takes the plank out of my eye so I can remove the speck in another's. Journal about it.

What do you need to put away judgment?

Circle one:

Hope

Fearlessness

Mercy

Love

God Glasses

Or write your own

CHAPTER 10

THE DAY ALL HELL BROKE LOOSE ON THE PLANE

I'd been flying for a few years and I'd learned so much. Sure, I made some rookie mistakes of forgetting to pray, and even my own bad attitude prevented me on many days from being full of peace and joy. God was so gracious that the majority of my flights were flown in peace in Jesus's name. Remember, it was THE FIRST THING God told me when I was called to be a flight attendant. He told me I could change the atmosphere of an airplane with his presence, and I'd seen him do it many times.

His Presence = Peace

I learned, by following the Holy Spirit's lead, how to take authority over the atmosphere: worship, decree God's word, pray, repeat.

So, my flights were MOSTLY peaceful. More and more, as I did the things above, I started believing and establishing God's peace. When I encountered medical emergencies, drama, etc, I adjusted. I started decreeing before the next trip that there would be none of that by God's grace. Only God's peace could enter the aircraft door. If something came on the plane, I learned how to introduce the chaos to meet its Maker, and everything would be required to bow to Jesus.

Some other FAs are good at, and built for, those "emergency" type of situations because they DO happen. God has called them to be there in those moments, but it just isn't why God has me on the plane. I can go back to that original call to carry His peace.

Unfortunately, last week was the exception. In fact, all hell broke loose on the plane.

4:10 AM sign in out of Portland. It was so early coffee places weren't even open. Jesus, help me.

I was assigned to the front of the aircraft. I cranked the worship music (just loud enough for me to hear) and began setting up the galley. As I always do, I was praying, decreeing, and worshiping as I worked.

During boarding, a woman claimed she was hot and needed to step off the airplane. It made sense. It was a teensy bit stuffy, and she was holding coffee. Man, I really wanted that coffee. I gave her a glass of ice water as she fidgeted outside the boarding door for a few minutes

As she came back on, I asked, "You okay, now?"

"Um, yes," and she rushed past me down the aisle.

Alrighty then. Ya meet all kinds on the plane.

We closed the door and began the taxi out with the safety demo playing on the monitors. I grabbed my phone and turned off my worship music as I always do when leaving the galley area. I heard in my spirit, "Leave the worship music on."

I clicked it off anyway, and I put my phone in my pocket. I thought that it couldn't be the Holy Spirit. I must be hearing things and a little loopy at this still very early hour.

I did my safety checks, and we buckled in for take-off. A woman came rushing down the aisle while the airplane is still rolling and about to go wheels up. I wave her back to her seat, but she's still barreling toward me.

It's the overheated coffee lady, except now she's not overheated, she's having a full-blown panic attack. "I can't do this. I just can't. I have to get off this plane. Now!"

I talked to her for a brief moment. I could tell it was likely anxiety, but she wanted off. I called the captain, "We have a woman who wants off the plane right now."

Thankfully, he was an understanding captain. "Copy."

I feel the airplane pull off to the side. We meandered back to our gate to let her off.

I started praying, "Jesus fix it. Peace. Peace. Peace."

We did the door closing and go through the procedures all over again. We finally were up in the air. A woman walks by me and snaps, "I don't like the way you're looking at me!" I was so confused! I mean, this is my face. She muttered, "Rude," to me as she walked off. This was turning out to be a strange flight.

As we began our descent, a different woman rang her call light repeatedly. The flight attendant in the back responded. I peeked around the corner. Yep, I remembered her. She'd been in and out of the potty for extended periods and leaving wafts of unpleasant smells in her wake. You notice these things when you have a seat right next to the lavatory door.

Curiously, she didn't fit the anxious flyer type, as a business woman in her creased pants and button down jacket. I knelt down in front of her. "You okay?" She says, "Something's not right. I don't feel right. I fly all the time. My hands are numb, and my head is tingling. I'm afraid I might go to sleep and never wake up." I was like, say what? Why would you go to sleep and not wake up?

We got her a cold compress, ice water. She refused to take oxygen or medical help on the plane, but she wanted the EMTs to meet us at the gate. I'm not a doctor so I wasn't sure exactly what was going on. If I had to guess, it sounded like anxiety with the tummy issues and the comment about not waking up.

I called the captain again. We are about to land, so now I have broken sterile cockpit two times (that's where the flight deck has to focus and is on Do Not Disturb). The captain's response was, "Copy." This guy! Compassionate saint. He was a man of few words, obviously. The only thing he said to me that morning when he got on the plane, "You have any trouble, don't hesitate to call." I dismissed that because I don't normally have trouble on flights, but wow, was I thankful for his support and calm demeanor. We landed and opened the door to allow the EMTs board. They loaded her up.

Whew! It was a rough flight, and I was glad it was over.

I was a little stressed for my next flight. Would it be more of the same? A woman boarded, and I greeted her. She immediately said, "You are friendlier than the friendly skies." Ahhh, what a kiss from God after my morning. I needed that hug from him.

WHAT I LEARNED

1. **Your presence matters.**
   The peace we carry from Heaven is as real as the wing on an airplane and able to keep us and others steady. Do all within God's power to deny boarding of your atmosphere to the enemy. When chaos comes, God has you in the palm of his hand.

2.   **We can't always use the same strategies and expect to be victorious.**
        Forget having a routine or formula. We have to follow moment by
        moment instructions: I SHOULD HAVE OBEYED AND KEPT THE
        WORSHIP MUSIC ON! WORSHIP IS A WEAPON. Jesus can fix it, but
        we must listen and obey.

3.   **A captain who will "copy" with support without frustration or
        argument showed me something about my Heavenly Captain.**
        God hears, cares, responds, and gets us all to safety. HE IS IN CHARGE,
        and his feathers don't get ruffled! Nothing surprises God. If you need
        anything, you can call on Him!

4.   **We have angelic help available to us.**
        We aren't supposed to pray to angels, but God has an army full of them.
        Next time, I will ask God for help from His angel armies. I needed it! This
        was too big for me. We are entering a season where we will need their
        help. They are a tool used to bring God's peace.

Life hack: Take His promises with you wherever you go. Look through God's
word and write His promises down on a note card to carry with you.

"The angel of the Lord encamps around those who fear Him, and rescues them."
Psalm 34:7, NASB

Question

What do you need to establish God's kingdom in your environment?
Journal about the peace of God on the following page.

Circle one:

Hope

Be a peace bringer

To study God's word

Worship

Or write your own

....

CHAPTER 11

IT'S ALL ABOUT SCIENCE, MAN

I was tempted to be disappointed as I looked at the trip I was assigned. I wanted to spend the evening with my husband, but it was an easy trip. A turn to Mexico. I would be back later that night.

I settled into the back row of the aircraft before boarding with my breakfast, and I turned on some worship music. I prayed for my trip and peace over the airplane.

My fellow flight attendant who was working in the back galley came on late. He was sweating bullets, so he grabbed a paper towel out of the lav and wiped the beads from his forehead and plump cheeks. I'll call him Christian.

Most guys I work with are gay, so I was surprised when he said his tardiness was because his wife had morning sickness.

Our conversation went along these lines:

He found out, on the week of Christmas, they were pregnant with their first child. He didn't believe he could have kids because he and his first wife tried for four years, so he felt like this child was a true "miracle."

I love to pray for babies. Christian was throwing the miracle word out there, so I asked if I could pray for his new little one.

Christian said, "Yeah. That would be great. I think my Mom is on her knees praying right now." I prayed for protection and that the baby would be hidden under the shadow of God's wing.

Well, imagine my surprise, after he so readily accepted the prayers of both myself and made mention of his mother's, when he said he was at times agnostic but mostly an atheist. He believed in science and the universe. I tried to make my face not look confused. I wanted to say, "Excuse me? God created that... You believe in the creation but not the creator?" But I know the tricks of the enemy, so I understand being deceived. I kept my thoughts to myself and said, "Well, thank you for sharing that. I'm glad you feel comfortable enough to be real and honest with me," and I meant it.

The flight was a little bumpy, so we stayed seated for a bit. I said some silent prayers.

Then, Christian began his, what we call in the airline biz, "jumpseat confession." It's true. People seriously tell you all kinds of crazy stories and confess their deepest darkest secrets on the jumpseat. You will more than likely never see the people you are flying with again at a big base like DFW, so why pay for a counselor? The jumpseat is a safe place to get it all out.

Christian grew up in a "cult" (his words). The church he attended followed the letter of the law. His mom didn't wear make-up, jewelry, or pants. They did not celebrate Christmas because it had become too commercialized, and they believed Jesus was born in the summer anyway. His denomination declared they, alone, were the Bride because they didn't indulge in any sort of worldly sin. Other people who believed in Jesus but sinned (like me) may get into a lower level of heaven (I'm so relieved). As for the rest, those who didn't believe, well, according to the church's leader, they were going to H-E double hockey sticks. Apparently, Christian went to a hell, fire, and brimstone kind of church.

The leader they followed was a self-appointed apostle of God, and he spoke the infallible truth. How can you argue with that?

Christian shared, "If the pastor wanted something from us, he started it with, "God says...." and then would back it up with scripture in some roundabout way. If you argued or didn't believe, then you were rebellious and 'out of fellowship.' The pastor preached extreme accountability, not necessarily to God, alone, but, also accountability to himself.

The church controlled Christian's family's life growing up.

The control even went so far that the leader had the password to all the member's bank accounts. If and when he saw fit, he could verify you were giving your obligatory 10%. If church members went to a non-Christian movie or were caught doing anything "worldly," they would be rebuked, and many were ostracized from the congregation for falling out of line with their idea of "holiness."

The pastor told Christian he could only marry someone within the church and only after securing the church's approval. There was a mandatory 3 step courtship process that the church was very involved in. No hand holding or one-on-one dates. As a teen, he was paired with a girl within the church. With the church's oversight and approval, he was married at nineteen. Christian said he'd never tasted a drop of alcohol, never cussed, and had kept himself pure in every way he knew how for his wife. His wife ended up leaving him and the church. She ended up going into the adult film industry.

As Christian walked through the painful process of his wife divorcing him, his pastor told him his only option was to remain single. He had one hope for companionship. His ex-spouse would have to come to her senses and return to him. So he prayed, and he waited for her.

Christian continued to attend church, but he was starting to notice things that didn't line up. He was weary of the overly controlling ways of the pastor twisting the scriptures. Christian was frustrated to be sentenced to this entire life alone unless he accepted someone back who had never truly loved him and had, in fact, betrayed him.

The pastor of the church became very ill. He continued to preach, not to worry, that he would be healed and/or raised up in the body of an eighteen-year-old young man. The church he attended believed in miraculous healing. Christian had even witnessed it for himself with a blind child's sight being restored. Still, Christian decided if the man died, then everything he believed about God was hogwash.

Well, the leader wasn't healed, and an eighteen-year-old guy never showed up to the pulpit claiming to be reincarnated, so Christian was done. He wanted out. He had lived a chaste life and done everything the "right way" to the letter of the law. Christian no longer believed any of it. He left the church. His family initially disowned him. He did some intense counseling and was now somewhat reconciled with his family. Christian remarried two years before our airplane ride. His wife was spiritual but didn't necessarily believe in one God, more in energies and light.

He told me, matter of factly, "For me, I believe in science and astronomy. Things that are provable rather than made up by a person. I've read the Bible, and I dedicated myself to it. I probably know the word better than most pastors. There's so much more out there, and religious people can't admit that you don't have all the answers. Admit it." He looked at me, "You don't know. You don't have all the answers."

I responded, "You're right. I don't have all of the answers. There are questions I have when I meet my maker. There are many things I don't understand."

Christian continued, "If you could just believe in something bigger than God based on facts! Earth is just this tiny speck in space. Space has been here for billions of years, and there's more to it. Science is where it's at. I'm telling you." He talked about how the universe was its own thing, and I listened not out of agreement but respect. He said, "You really need to think about this."

To be an atheist, someone had to consider once that there was a God to determine they didn't believe He existed. I've noticed that most atheists have reached out to God, and they didn't get the answer they expected, or, like Christian, they were very hurt by the church and walked away.

I had no answer for many of the things he brought up with science that, in his mind, refuted the validity of the Bible. Jesus followers like to be the only ones sharing their reality and views, but we don't know how to listen and hear the heart like Jesus did. We say things without asking the Holy Spirit first, so I've learned to zip it unless God creates the opportunity. It would have been lovely for God to give me something profound to say. Maybe God should have made me some practiced apologist who could argue for their faith? I have faith, and I know what I believe because it's in my heart. Because He shows me in little ways on a daily basis, because I believe His word is true and, because even when I was far away from Him, He never gave up on me.I had an undeniable encounter with God. It changed me forever. No one can ever talk me out of my own first hand experience.

When I'm on a Holy Spirit adventure, arguing and pushing my beliefs doesn't feel like the Father's heart to me. I don't want to argue with anyone about God. Can you see God saying, "Yeah, and tell him this! I'm right, and he's wrong, and this is why." No, the Father's heart sounds to me something like, "I know you've been hurt by those who claimed to represent me. I miss you. I love you. We can work through this if you will give our relationship another try."

I listened to Christian, and I prayed. I asked the Holy Spirit how to handle this. Christian was obviously trying to convert me to his way of thinking.

I felt led to respond, "See, what you are talking about takes more faith for me than believing in God. For me, science is us trying to explain God, which we can't. Believing that we all got here by some accident doesn't make sense to me. The rules of gravity, the laws of the universe, they point to an engineer, a creator. Someone had to set it up, right?"

Christian then told me he understood engineering because, on the side, he was a software engineer. Wow! Doesn't God have the best way to reach a heart without arguing? God spoke to him about an engineer. Christian knew I didn't know that fact about him.

A passenger rang their call light, so I excused myself. When I got back, he immediately apologized, "I'm sorry. I was pushing my science on you and my beliefs. My parents are still very much part of the church, and my dad is an elder. We've come to an agreement that I won't push them, and they won't push me, so I can't believe I did that. I just flew with another flight attendant. She was a Christian, and she drove me crazy. She used every hour of the 3-day trip to try to show me how wrong I was and how right she was. I have these conversations all the time with people, and I'm usually not pushy, so please forgive me."

I responded, "Of course. You are not being pushy. I'm all in with God. There's no turning back for me. There came a point where I pushed all my chips into the center of the table. He's mine, and I am His, so please don't worry about being pushy with me. I'm just glad you feel safe enough to share your thoughts with me."

We finished our first flight and loaded back up to head home. We were about to do our service, so the flight attendant who sits up front came back to help. We were waiting on Christian to finish setting up the cart. With no knowledge of my earlier conversation with Christian, the other flight attendant starts chatting it up and talking about her new church. She tells us both that she left the church she attended since birth because they were controlling. She thought it was so wrong that you needed a priest to be an intermediary between you and God. She swore she would never step foot in another church because of her father's abuse towards her mother. The church didn't help her mom when she needed it most. Her mom had married a protestant, so she was on her own according to the church. The flight attendant said she was done with church but not God. Then, her mom asked her to try a non-denominational church and she loved it.

I mean, you cannot make this stuff up. Christian knew the other flight attendant had no way of knowing what he and I were talking about earlier. I felt she was there for back up, spiritually speaking. I didn't have to have all the right answers. He showed Christian in a very profound way that bad church experiences could be overcome if Christian wanted to give it another try.

I prayed and prayed whether I should say anything else or remain silent. Usually, God speaks through me without my brain consciously realizing it is Him, like about the engineering thing, or sometimes, when I tell a story, it will speak to their heart, but I wasn't sensing anything. We stayed bobbing on the surface now with our conversations.

A question popped into my spirit to ask Christian. It was at the end of our last flight, and the last few passengers were deplaning. I said, "Would you do me a favor about God? You don't have to. I mean..."

Christian interrupted, "Yes, I'll do it. What is it? Ask anything. I was horrible to you."

"Will you ask God about how your baby was made? How he created him? Where your baby's soul came from?"

"So you want Him to prove to me..."

I interjected, "No! I promise I don't have some agenda with that question or preconceived right answer in my head, and, honestly, I don't know what He will say, but would you be willing to ask?"

"Yes, I will! And then maybe we will fly together, and I can share it with you?"

"That would be great ," I said.

So rather than being offended at each other's differences, we were totally cool. We were two radically different, polar opposite believers. He believed in "science," and I believed in Jesus. On the surface, we had nothing in common, but we walked off the plane as respectful seekers of God's truth. Maybe we will meet again, and his faith in a loving (not controlling) God will be restored.

A few things to ponder when you encounter resistance from another person when trying to share your faith:

DOUBT
Can we all admit we've had times of doubt? Especially when our circumstances don't line up with His promises? I've asked questions like: Are you real? Do you care about me? Those times would really confuse me, but now I don't get too much into my head or try to figure things out. I ask God questions, and if I wait, He answers me through a sermon, a devotional, the Bible, sometimes a secular movie or song (gasp), or He's even used a billboard sign! We can empathize with people who struggle with doubt if we are honest.

LISTEN
We can listen respectfully and respond with authenticity. Religion caused Christian a great deal of pain and heartache. I have no idea the depth of that pain and the loneliness he felt when his wife cheated on him or the isolation he felt when his family rejected him. The least I can do is hear his heart, his hurts and his reasons "why." In the past, I would be so freaked out that I wouldn't be able to have these types of conversations without getting judgmental, defensive, or simply shutting down and walking away. With the Holy Spirit's counsel, God has taught me to listen. Really listen to another's heart and not poo-poo on their beliefs or be disrespectful. I ask the Holy Spirit to speak through me and, sometimes, that means saying NOTHING. I don't have to have

all the right answers. Pray and be sensitive to what He is saying and let God do what only He can.

"Before I formed you in the womb I knew you, before you were born I set you apart; I appointed you as a prophet to the nations."
Jeremiah 1:5, NIV

Question

Test out your gift of prophecy by asking God how He sees the person in front of you. Journal about it and ask Him if you should share.

What do you need to be a better listener?

Circle one:

To pray it instead of say it

Peace

Love

A deeper connection with God

Patience

Or write your own

....

CHAPTER 12

WHEN IT DOESN'T GO WELL

In San Antonio at a coffee shop for the free WiFi. The coffee shop was crowded, and I happened to score a sweet spot right next to the electrical outlet.

A guy came in and kind of wandered around like a lost puppy. All the tables were taken. I ignored him and spread things out a little bit on the table to mark my territory. Still, he asked if he could sit in the chair across from me. At first, I was a little put out. Earbuds in. Can't you see I'm busy and can't be bothered right now?

The funny part about all this was I had a ball cap with a rhinestone cross on my head right before he walked in. I randomly took it off even though my hair sticks up like alfalfa when I don't wash it. I was on day three or four, maybe, of no-wash, but I took the hat off and put it in my bag for an unknown reason. (You will notice, in hindsight, on Holy Spirit adventures, how you are being led by God.)

As he sat down, I instantly knew the Holy Spirit led him to sit in that very chair. I took my earbuds out and asked God to lead. The pleasantries were exchanged: His name was Ernie, a professor at the University of Texas at San Antonio. He was open and conversational, but we were both busy on our respective computers. From a few sentences, I could tell I wasn't Ernie's type. My mustache probably is not quite thick enough for his taste. I think you're picking up what I'm putting down. He held same sex attractions.

I was having this running conversation in my head with God about Ernie. I felt like God said so many wonderful things about him. The Holy Spirit said Ernie was creative, influenced many, and he was a linch pin that held things together. He was a teacher, so that all made sense. I also heard that he was an integral part of God's plan, but the last thing God said to me was "tragic end." When I heard that, it really hurt my heart.

Unfortunately, during the conversation in my head, I watched Ernie squint to read the Christian bumper sticker on the back of my computer. It's quite large and has a cross on it with a scripture. Many people have come to talk to me because it is a beacon of hope for them. Well, it was not a beacon of hope for Ernie. As he read it, his face turned from relaxed and open to a full-out grimace. He looked like I had personally offended him with it. His horror was that obvious. Ernie shut down as quickly as my son does when I ask him what he's feeling inside. Ernie fiddled and looked quickly around as if to say, "get me out of here. She's a Christian!" I tried to keep my hands in the open where he could see them... I didn't have a Bible to beat over his head or a nifty brochure with ten things you need to stop doing for Jesus to love you. I hadn't even mentioned Jesus, yet.

He looked around the coffee shop, and relief flashed when he saw a table open up. He quickly grabbed his things calling "Bye!" over his shoulder. I seriously don't think he could get away fast enough.

I was headed to an art museum a few blocks away. I stopped outside the coffee shop, and I prayed for Ernie. I hated hearing "tragic end" and leaving things undone, but that door was VERY clearly closed. It was, in fact, barred by Ernie.

While I was praying, I caught sight of Ernie crossing the street. I wanted to go after him, but I asked the Holy Spirit and didn't feel a nudge. I was glad because I didn't want to be a Christian stalker. I walked the opposite direction towards the art museum, bummed. I was sad for Ernie and thought maybe I didn't get to accomplish, in that brief time, what God intended, but I asked God to send more help.

When I was walking back to my hotel later, I couldn't believe it. There, in front of me, was Ernie again. He was hard to miss in his hot pink shirt, and blue jean cut-off shorts. What are the odds? I had walked a mile to the coffee shop and that was hours ago. I'm willing to look foolish when God gives me a confirmation like that! I prayed and then called out hello to him as he came towards me, and he said briskly, "Oh, it's you. Hello." He was power walking. His plan was pretty clear to steer clear of the crazy Christian bumper sticker girl with the now blinged-out cross on her head.

I knew God had designed the first meeting as well as this one, and Ernie had shown up, so that said something! I said, "Hey, sometimes God has me run into someone, and it's a divine appointment because he wants me to deliver a message. Do you want me to ask and see what he has to say?"

He said, "Oh, I think it was all just a coincidence. I was just waiting for an open table, and now I'm out taking a walk."

So, basically, NO, Ernie wasn't interested in hearing what I had to say.

I'm not deterred easily when I feel Holy Spirit urges, and if God's angels went through this much trouble to get us here at this moment AGAIN then I was going to do my part... So, I said, "Then, can I give you a hug?"

He said reluctantly, "Well, ok."

I know in my spirit that the encounter did not have the outcome that was the highest and best. Ha! To say the least. I looked like a crazy Christian stalker but, unlike Ernie, I don't believe in coincidences. This was a divine appointment. I shared this interaction with a friend and asked for her wisdom. She said she sensed Plan A was Ernie opening his heart to be touched at our shared table. Plan B was for him to receive what God had to say, which Ernie politely declined. Plan C was the hug. I know part of my mission is to find God's lost sheep, His children, and plant seeds of love and truth.

As I processed the situation with Jesus, I felt specifically Ernie's grandfather had prayed for us to have this conversation. But I think Ernie's offense and fear of Christians put up a wall. The Spirit within Ernie was willing. It delivered him to my table, and it actually delivered him to meet me again on the river walk, but Ernie, or maybe his fear, would not open the door to his heart: God was knocking through me. God is greater and stronger than fear, but He will not override our free will. He's so gentle... but He is also a persistent knocker.

This interaction has haunted me a little. I felt the gravity of Ernie's life (tragic end) and how he will feel when he leaves the earth as we all will... His choice to refuse to open the door to his heart, but that is FEARFUL thinking. I realized that his receipt of a hug actually might have been Ernie looking through the peephole and considering unlocking the door to God. God will send someone else after me to call out gently until Ernie is ready and knows it's safe to open the door. I pray that someday Ernie will let God in. I would do everything in my power to have a relationship with my children. God will continue to knock until He can't knock anymore. His love is unstoppable.

"And He said to them, 'I watched Satan fall from heaven like lightning.'"
Luke 10:18, ESV

Question

Do you want to practice hearing from the Holy Spirit? During your conversations, take a moment to ask the Holy Spirit what He is doing or what He wants to say. Then be brave and do it!

What do I need from God to go on my own Holy Spirit adventure?

Circle one:

Boldness

Favor

A day of peace

God to carry my burdens

Gift of prophecy

Word of knowledge

Or write your own

CHAPTER 13

CRASH & BURN

On a three leg day with two more flights to go. We were getting a new flight deck crew. The captain and first officer came on board and introduced themselves.

I said, "I have two bottles of water. Do you guys need anything else?"

The first officer chimed in, "Do you have any of that good ice cream?"

"Ah no... it was a short flight in, so all we have is the snack basket."

The captain stood between me and the first officer. He looked around and leaned in saying quietly, "You know, I had a flight attendant tell me one time that it's like a bl__ job. If you have to ask for it, you probably aren't going to get it." He laughed loudly at his own joke. The first officer seemed embarrassed and ducked into the cockpit.

I call this fishing. I ignored the captain's bait, and WITHOUT a smile, I said, "I guess you'll have water then." If I called him out on what he said with an "Excuse me?" he would say he's joking, didn't mean anything by it, lighten up. After all, he was just repeating what a FLIGHT ATTENDANT told him.

With my lack of response to his unappreciated and unwanted joke, you would think the captain would get the hint but, no, it didn't seem so when he continued on, "Hey, it looks like we are with you guys through tomorrow. Drinks and dinner are on me tonight at the hotel. Whatever you want."

I said nothing for a minute. "I brought my dinner with me. My husband usually makes it." I wanted to make it clear that I wanted no part in this. I was married, and so was he.

He looked flustered, "Oh, okay...and umm, you are welcome to share that with the rest of the crew too." And then he finally gets it. I'm not gonna be lured in.

I said, "They are all in the back if you want to ask."

One time, a pilot wanted to show me a picture of himself in a costume on his phone. He had gone to the Burning Man Festival. At least he forewarned me, "It's kind of a hedonistic festival, so the picture is a little off-color." I put my hand up and do what flight attendants call the "international stop sign." I quickly told him, "Then please put that away. I don't want to see those types of things." Another pilot once told me how beautiful my eyes were and repeatedly called me "blue eyes." I ignored him completely until he used my actual NAME. I'm here to work with you on a team. Another asks me if he can help me check the equipment "Since you're in a skirt." No! That will not be necessary. There are older men who hit on the way, way too young for them, new hires. I've learned to be respectful but still point out the inappropriateness, "That's really thoughtful of you to ask, since she could be your granddaughter."

Once a pilot asked me why I wouldn't go to a simple dinner. I said, "Out of respect for my husband, I just don't." He knew I was a new hire, and said, "I'll give you six months, and you'll be going out." I never have.

You may think that's unreasonable, but it's what my husband and I decided together for both of us. You see, simple dinners can become something more. We know how to end a marriage, because we have both done things not honoring in our past when it involved the opposite sex. Trust was broken for both of us. We were divorced over them and then reconciled seven years later. Because of that, we take extra precautions that might seem excessive to others, but it's what we've decided to do.

At first, when I started working, I felt so on guard because of my past but, I was also still tempted at times when I felt lonely. If there is some lack of connection at home and if there is a lack in our own integrity, then these two things can lead to marital amnesia. We can forget we have made a lifelong covenant. But because of my history, I have given the Holy Spirit permission to remind me to RUN.

I have a journal where I pray over the cities I visit, and at the very back, I have a list of pilots' names who, by my standards, have been not been honoring to me. I ask God to wake them up and convict their hearts. I pray while they bring a whole airplane full of people safely to their destination, their own family would not crash and burn. I could tell you stories of how I prayed these prayers, and the next day, while flying, the person I prayed for was completely different and even repentant in their demeanor.

One pilot came on the next day after I had prayed for him. He was so humble and said he hadn't slept well all night because he'd been thinking about the meaning of his life. The day before, he had really trash-talked his wife in front of us. He had an unusual last name and said his wife had a stripper's name. Again, joking but not a nice thing to say about his precious wife. It's amazing how, because of my background, I don't condemn but pray for conviction. I know it makes a way for Him to speak to their hearts. Of course, they can ignore it, but at least their eyes are opened to the truth of their behavior. These aren't evil men. They are children of God, and they have lost their way and need help to see the light. Writing this has caused me to realize I could have prayed more about it, but it's such an uncomfortable situation. I don't like thinking about it very much. I don't want to give the wrong impression. I could have ten flight deck crews with zero issues, but that one bad experience stays with me. A friend of mine told me, "We are all one tempting situation from blowing up our life."

Even when I have been on Holy Spirit adventures, I've had the fear and the thought that people might think that I am flirting or it could open a door for something inappropriate with the opposite sex. It's a very good idea to have defined boundaries. When I first began stepping out in the gift of prophecy, I noticed that I would get a lot of words for men. We really have to check ourselves in this area and ask God for purity of heart. God showed me this was a hole in my heart and a desire to connect with men because, over my life, I've often felt a lack of connection with my own father. I walked through repentance and a process of submitting this area of my life to God. Now, I can honestly say if I do get a word for a gentleman, it's from a place of purity and not a personal need.

Are you struggling with this, or is there a fear you have of being on a Holy Spirit adventure and people getting the wrong idea? Do you feel impure motives in your heart when stepping out in the gifts God has given you?

If you feel led, you can say this prayer:

Jesus, I ask you to purify my heart and motives. I repent of any way that I've used your name or the missions you've sent me on or the interactions I've had as opportunities to satisfy or feed my flesh. I receive your forgiveness, and thank you that you carried my shame on the cross. It is a gift for you to reveal areas so I can be made clean by you. Jesus, I submit myself to you to reveal anything you want to remove from my life, and I ask that you take it from me until I look like you. Until I only do what the Father does and only say what He does in Jesus's name and by His power, I pray. Amen.

"Search me, O God, and know my heart; test my thoughts. Point out anything you find in me that makes you sad, and lead me along the path of everlasting life."
Psalm 139:23-24, TLB

"Therefore let the one who thinks he stands firm [immune to temptation, being overconfident and self-righteous], take care that he does not fall into sin and condemnation."
1 Corinthians 10:12, AMP

Question

What do I need from Jesus today to be made clean:

Circle one:

Forgiveness

Hope

Shame removed

Love

Motives revealed to my heart

Or write your own

....

CHAPTER 14

BROTHERLY LOVE

I was in Philly, and a crew of precious young people surrounded me and asked me if they could pray for me. Then, they took my prayer request and nailed it to a huge cross! It was such a sweet set up because then I was able to ask them if they needed prayer. I prayed for them and called out destiny. I may not know the fruit until Heaven, but it is so much fun when these little God kisses occur. Be ready to bless on your adventures with the Holy Spirit but also be prepared to receive blessings! We have the gift of encouraging, and we are encouraged by other believers.

This reminds me of a song by Hezekiah Walker:

I need you, you need me.
We're all a part of God's body.
Stand with me, agree with me.
We're all a part of God's body.
I pray for you, You pray for me.
I love you, I need you to survive.
I won't harm you with words from my mouth.
I love you, I need you to survive.

It's so fun to be God's hands and feet, but it is also a blessing to be part of someone else's Holy Spirit-led adventure.

"Therefore encourage one another and build up one another, just as you also are doing."
1 Thessalonians 5:11, NLT

Question

Are you more comfortable praying for others than receiving prayer?

What do you need to receive from others?

Circle one:

Transparency

Hope

Humility

Walls crumble in Jesus name

Or write your own

....

CHAPTER 15

LOST

I was on a layover in Austin and found myself having trouble navigating to a bakery. I stopped in the street and looked down at my phone, and looked up. I thought, "No, the bakery is that direction." I looked at the sun. It rises in the east and sets in the west. I'm 99% sure of that.

I pass a young guy, just a kid really, putting change in the parking meter. I heard in my head, "God's not done with him yet."

I kept walking. Thanks for sharing, God.

"Tell him."

I don't really know where I am right now and Juanita, (That's Wanna-eat-a), my alter personality that emerges when I'm hungry, was getting hangry.

Juanita pressed me on past the guy, and I kept trucking down the street to find my delicious and flaky croissant.

I argued with the voice that was calling me back to him. "It's not safe," I said out loud. What if this guy is a predator who will chop me up into tiny pieces... put me in the trunk of that car he's parking, or what if he thinks I'm going to ask him for money or chop HIM into little pieces. I was definitely overthinking it and getting frustrated. Juanita wasn't in the best of moods.

I passed a beautiful and very intimidating dog being walked by its' owner. God was showing me He had guard dogs to protect me. I didn't need to be afraid. I was out of real excuses.

This question popped up in my spirit, "What if you are the only person who will give him this message?"

I shushed Juanita's fussy "But I'm hungry!" argument. I thought of all the work that would go into getting this young man to be here at this exact place at this precise moment where our paths would intersect on this Holy Spirit adventure like with Ernie and Jacob in the previous chapters. I looked back, and the guy was still fiddling with the parking meter. (I think God's angels may have had a hand in a meter malfunction to stall him;) The dog was off the leash now and standing right behind the guy. Not a great guard dog.

I stopped and said to God, "Okay, I'll do it." I turned around and walked quickly back so I wouldn't chicken out.

"Err...Excuse me...um... sorry. Hi." I startled the guy, and he jumped. He was scared of me! "I was walking by and felt God wanted me to give you a message, if that's okay?"

He didn't say yes, but he didn't say no and dipped his head in a slightly confused nod, "God said that he's not done with you yet." More flowed out from the Holy Spirit as I obeyed with the first part, "Your future days will be better than your former days. Don't give up. You can begin again today. Try again. It will be different now."

The guy smiled a huge smile and said, "God said that about me?"

"Yep. God bless you and have a great rest of your day."

"Thank you so much, and God bless you," he called out as we parted.

And it was done. Message delivered. God didn't share details about why the guy needed a new beginning, but maybe he'd been geographically challenged on God's path for his life and needed that encouragement.

I wonder how many other people God puts on my path that need a word from Him? I felt a little more dependent and open to His voice since I was in an unfamiliar territory and struggling with direction. I've noticed that, when I'm out of my comfort zone, I hear more clearly because I'm off auto pilot.

Maybe He places people on our path that need to hear from Him more than we realize, but we are too busy or distracted. Our focus is on ourselves and our own agenda rather than what God has planned for us and our day. Be open to His gentle nudges today. Please share your divine encounter with a friend. It encourages people to go on their own adventures with the Holy Spirit.

"Instead, encourage each other every day, as long as it's called "today," so that none of you become insensitive to God because of sin's deception."
Hebrews 3:13, CEB

Question

What do I need from the Holy Spirit to focus on God's agenda today?

Circle One:

Submission moment by moment

God to lift my burdens

Awareness

Ears to hear

A soft heart

Or write your own

....

CHAPTER 16

FEARFUL

A fellow flight attendant, Derek, was scrolling through his news feed on the plane as we waited for passengers to board.

"Big day for news," Derek says.

"Really? What's up?"

"Four different terrorist attacks."

"That's terrible."

"... and the Supreme Court is supposed to rule on equality for marriage."

"How do you feel about that?" I asked Derek.

"Well, it is pretty big news."

Derek had smoothly avoided my question.

Derek and I talked while I worked. I surmised, based on our discussion, that Derek was romantically interested in men.

I am sure Derek knew within five minutes of working with me that I loved Jesus. The Jesus bling cross that hung around my neck was technically against uniform code, the worship music, and the presence of God that is inside me can be felt, I know.

I paused and then felt a nudge from the Holy Spirit to press a bit further, "What would you like to see happen from the Supreme Court?"

"Oh, I don't know." He changed the subject AGAIN and began talking about politics, national news, presidential candidates but stayed on the surface without a personal commitment.

I said, "Have you ever thought about going into politics?"

He responded, "I don't think I could ever do that."

"It sounds like you are very interested in it."

"I just couldn't... Because I know what I think in my head, but it's really hard to put it into words. I don't want to argue with anyone."

Ahhh, so that was why he wouldn't answer my question directly. He thought I would argue with him.

I have a lot of time to myself when I travel, so that night in my hotel room, I prayed for Derek along the following lines, "God, please help Derek communicate what is in his heart and for him to feel Your love. Amen."

After I prayed, I saw a picture in my mind. Derek was crying. His arms were up in front of his face in protection. He was pleading, "Please, please don't be mean to me." I felt a rush of love for Derek and God's tenderness towards him. I felt like God said, "I would never be mean to Derek."

Funny thing, when I don't deliver God's messages, I find that my flight gets delayed. Isn't God sweet for giving me extra time to deliver His messages?

HA!

So I've learned to ask the Holy Spirit if it's a message that needs to be delivered. I will see a green light or a red light. Red lights mean whatever I hear or see or even know from God's word, I am to commit to prayer only. God leads us to speak the right word at the right time. Sometimes, He calls us to be silent.

As I got on the plane, I checked in with the Holy Spirit. The lights were all green, and I wanted to get home on time, so before our first flight that day, I promptly said, "Derek, as you know, I'm a praying momma, so I said a little prayer for you last night. God said the sweetest thing. Do you want to hear what I felt like I heard from God for you?"

"Um. Well. Sure," he said hesitantly. His face looked so vulnerable, like that of a little boy.

"I felt like God said, "I would never be mean to Derek.""

He looked down and said, "Thanks so much," and kept looking at his hands. He was swallowing. I thought he might be fighting back tears.

I didn't follow it up with, "Oh, and, hey, stop being gay," because that's not what God told me to say.

Instead, I continued, "Isn't God so kind to say that? He loves you so much and is a good Father to you. I was physically abused as a kid, and it took a long time for me to accept that God is not going to punish me. I thought God was angry, but He's always been so gentle and loving to me even in his discipline, and He is gentle with you too."

Derek looked up and nodded. He seemed to be released to be himself from that exchange, and he was way more chatty. Randomly, throughout the day, Derek told me three different stories where passengers had verbally assaulted him, and one had been met by the police at the airport. It was like in telling his stories, Derek was being unburdened as well as healed of his worst fear, people being mean to him. God's message of loving-kindness can disarm the enemy.

I pray that God opens Derek's heart to experience the fullness of his heavenly Father's love. I pray for Derek's freedom and deliverance from all that holds him back from being who God created him to be.

THE MORAL OF THE STORY

We may think someone has to "fix" something before they are lovable, but He loved us first even in our sin, yes, even then. He loved us as a father loves his precious child.

"Gracious words are like a honeycomb, sweetness to the soul and health to the body."
Proverbs 16:24, ESV

"Such love has no fear because perfect love expels all fear. If we are afraid, it is for fear of punishment, and this shows that we have not fully experienced his perfect love."
1 John 4:18, NLT

Question

We know God loved us when we were not perfect, so what do we need from the Holy Spirit to have faith and love those who don't live according to God's word currently?

Circle one:

Compassion

Love

Eyes to see

Peace

Freedom

A heart like God

Or write your own

....

CHAPTER 17

THE SWEATY GUY AND TWO EMOTIONAL SUPPORT ANIMALS

I was working first-class, and the agent came down to ask if we could pre-board a lady and her TWO emotional support dogs. Welp, I love doggies, and so did one of the other flight attendants, so we gave the thumbs up.

A young twenty-something year old girl got on with her college sorority shirt and yoga pants with her two Shih Tzu dogs. They weren't big dogs, but they weren't teeny tiny either. I gave the pup-pups some love. I asked her politely to put her bags up in the overhead bin when she had an opportunity since there was no storage in front of her seat.

She waved her hand and said, "Can you tell me if this seat is empty so I can have some more room? There's not enough room."

Hmmm.

What I wanted to say: You are able to purchase an additional seat if needed. If you want to talk about no room, you should try coach seating. A spirit of thankful would come upon you! Ha! But, instead, I kept it simple.

"I'll check, but first-class will likely be full."

"Oh, great," she said sarcastically.

Oh, lawd. It's going to be a long flight to LA. She opens her suitcase and puts it in the currently open seat next to her.

I wasn't sure if she missed my, "First-class will likely be full," or that she needed to put her three bags UP. Not to mention, her "emotional support" dogs were crawling everywhere. I'd let it ride for a minute. It was unlikely, but possible, the seat would be open.

I forgot about her and her problems. I began setting up my galley and getting pre-departure drink stuff ready when she slams the bathroom door open next to me with a flurry of expletives. She had one dog under her arm as she fumed, "This purse is probably ruined."

I say commiseratively, "It's hard traveling with little ones. Probably like traveling with kids."

"It's not the dogs. That dumba** spilled my Starbucks all over my $1000 Louis Vuitton."

Wait. Where was her other dog?

I peeked around the corner to her seat. I cannot paint this picture for you with words, but I will try. An Asian businessman with Harry Potter glasses is sitting in the seat next to her seat. HER suitcase is in front of HIS knees. His briefcase in his lap, with hands clutched on the top handle. Eyes straight forward. He is sweating bullets while HER other dog is on the armrest sniffing and licking the guy's ear.

I looked at her. Okay, so THIS guy spilled YOUR Starbucks? There was a lot of entitlement going on. She could care less how she was affecting those around her.

The other flight attendant put the girl's bag up that was still in the aisle.

I asked her seatmate, "Would you like me to put your briefcase up? He nodded but didn't let go. I shooed the dog out of his ear, but he'd already bonded with the guy and likely considered him a new friend.

The guy reluctantly released the briefcase that he was holding onto like a life preserver.

The young girl huffed around the corner, "Where's my suitcase?"

"We had to put it up to make room for the other passengers."

"Well, I needed something out of it!"

"Can it wait until after we take off? And if you could please keep the doggies close to you."

"I guess."

She was a mess the whole flight. The guy next to her was obviously traumatized. I'm not sure if she yelled at him about her Starbucks (not his fault). The guy sat the ENTIRE three-hour flight and refused everything. He said no to water, nuts, meal, dessert. He had now pressed himself to the very opposite edge of his seat away from her, and he looked like he might need some emotional support after this ride.

I tell this story for two reasons – First, because it is HILARIOUS. Just when you think you've seen it all on the airplane, something like this happens, but also because many of my Holy Spirit adventures were, and still are, about revealing life lessons.

This scenario is the dynamic for a lot of people in life. We work around high maintenance drama people who are entitled or very self-focused or maybe extra needy folks, or we are them.

It was a reminder to me. Don't play these parts in life: the demanding, needy, self-focused part or the silent victim.

We don't have to allow others to covertly put their drama, pushiness or problems, and sense of entitlement on us. Their drama spills over into our realm without a please, thank you, or would you consider helping me with this. We can also, either rush in to help, or we sit silently sweating and shut down until we blow up and cut off the relationship. We have every right to say kindly, "Hey, can we have a dividing line that represents our seat areas...a plan to separate your chaos and mine?"

When my freedom encroaches and affects you, then it's okay for you to say so and vice versa. Otherwise, we perpetuate this fallacy about relationships; that only one person matters.

The Holy Spirit is no pushover, and it's okay to speak up when we feel like we are in an unrighteous situation. Being loving in the name of Jesus can slip into being an enabler, co-dependency, or people-pleasing. Be gentle with one another, but speak your piece and bring God's peace.

"With patience, a ruler may be won over, and a gentle tongue can break bones."
Proverbs 25:15, CJB

Question

Do you see yourself in this scenario? Always being the one who has a lot of needs that only other people can satisfy? Maybe you find yourself wanting to push your way? Or do you identify more as the silent suffering type who can and should use your voice to speak God's loving truth?

What do we need from God to be led by the Holy Spirit in these situations?

Circle one:

Courage

Wisdom

Love

Truth

Boldness

Or write your own

....

CHAPTER 18

SAINT ANTONIO

While sitting at the DFW airport, I was surrounded by what looked to be a full military troop dressed in fatigues. Storms had rolled in, and we weren't going anywhere for the moment. I couldn't find a plug for my phone charger, so I asked one of the soldiers if he would mind sharing the other plug on his outlet. While we sat, I asked his name and about his life. He told me his name was Antonio, and he was on his way to San Antonio for basic training. While writing this, I find it interesting that his name was part of the city he was traveling to, and that city, San Antonio, was also named after a Saint. I love seeing the connections of God at work.

I felt it in my heart. A prayer opportunity had presented itself. I asked for Antonio's permission to pray, and he readily agreed. Antonio shared his father was a pastor. I prayed that Antonio would be bulletproof and that God would guide his steps. I also prayed he would be a leader for God and share his faith and shine God's light into the darkest of places.

I gave Antonio the devotional I was reading out of my bag: "My Utmost for His Highest." It seemed to be the perfect gift for someone who was willing to give his utmost for God and his fellow man. Antonio said, "Thank you. I definitely believe in the power of prayer."

Antonio's face looked a little anxious. I looked around at the whole crew of fifty-sixty guys at the gate waiting for the flight. They all looked a little lost. Just a bunch of brave kids who will need a heavenly Father's helping hand and his voice to guide them as they leave their families.

Funny, after our prayer, I got re-routed to San Antonio on the next flight. God had boots on the ground there, both physically and spiritually. Will you say a prayer for Antonio and the young men who are in our military willing to lay down their lives so we can have a safe place to live?

It's such a sweet thing to be a part of God's plan and pray for his honorable ones.

WHAT I LEARNED

Be open to the Holy Spirit creating opportunities like this for you. If there were any other outlets open, I would have used them and probably avoided the group. God knows how to create the situations and bring us to the right place at the right time. We only have to be willing to be led by Him and say what he tells us to say. I could have gotten frustrated at the storms, the crowded airport and huffed off and been in my head about it. The more you see the goodness that comes out of unwanted or unexpected situations, the more you can have enough peace during them to stay sensitive to what God is doing. Sometimes, the setbacks are actually setups!

"And how will they preach unless they are commissioned and sent [for that purpose]? Just as it is written and forever remains written, "How beautiful are the feet of those who bring good news of good things!"
Romans 10:15, AMP

Question

What do you need to be led by the Holy Spirit and aware of these God moments and opportunities?

Circle one:

Awareness

Peace

Love in my heart

Boldness

Or write your own

....

CHAPTER 19

HELPFUL

The evening before had been rough. A hot airplane, a three-hour delay, and too many fussy passengers. One lady actually said, "You, flight attendants, are the most inattentive and unhelpful people I have ever met!"

"I'm sorry," I wanted to snap back, "Was I unhelpful when I put your 3-year-old on the toilet as you asked me to while you held your other baby? Was I inattentive when I brought your family the five glasses of water and a cup of ice during our delay?" This is a true story. You might have noticed that entitled people get to me, and I forget the scripture, "Work willingly at whatever you do, as though you were working for the Lord rather than for people." Colossians 3:23, NLT. I'm still in process on my love walk.

The next morning, after six hours of sleep, I walked on to the airplane, and the air conditioning was still malfunctioning. Was it going to be another bad day? When things were tough on the airplane, I have to purposely ask God to help me think His way. I put my worship music on and tried to feel that peace that I so longed to feel from God. I asked Him to help me.

Two flight attendants came back to the galley. "We're on the jumpseat!" That would mean five people in an airplane galley. It would be like a clown car. I was not well-rested. It felt like things weren't going my way, and I fought the urge to check out mentally.

We began our service, and I did my best to serve everyone and be upbeat, but I was going through the motions. My heart felt cold and detached. The lady's words from the day before hung over me like a black cloud. "Unhelpful." I knew I would be of no use to God in my current state. To be honest, I felt so oppressed by my circumstances. It was hard not to feel sorry for myself. I was away from my family and doing His work, but no one was grateful. I was tired, and He didn't seem to be intervening even though I'd asked.

I've included many beautiful and miraculous stories in the book. I don't want you to be discouraged if you step out and things are challenging. Some days things don't go as planned, but He is building our endurance. God does hear our prayers and cries for help. He is full of help.

I noticed one of the young flight attendants (a jumpseater) was reading a book about faith that I recognized called "The Case for Christ." She told me about her fairly recent encounter with God. We started chatting about Jesus. I felt the black cloud of negativity lifting as we lifted Jesus' name higher.

Every time I looked at this young flight attendant my eyes welled up with tears. I love when that happens. He lets me feel his heart for another. He adored this young woman. I had an overwhelming sense of a heavenly Father's pride as she talked about the things she had walked away from because it wouldn't bring her closer to God. Specifically, she let go of any guys where she would be "missionary dating." (trying to lead them to Christ)

She made the following declaration, and it was so powerful to me: "I told God I don't want anything or anyone in my life that will come between me and You." This girl was ALL IN. It took me so long to say that in my own walk with God and really follow through. Her fiery love for God lit up the waning embers of my own heart.

I asked her if there was anything I could pray for her about. She said she didn't worry about a lot of things anymore, but she worried about her family. She felt some separation from her family because of her conversion and newfound faith in Jesus. Her family members were not believers, and she explained that she didn't know the Bible well enough to share why she believed what she believed.

I understood. When I first became a Christian, I scoured the scriptures and tried to learn them well. The Bible says, "...Always be prepared to give an answer to everyone who asks you to give the reason for the hope that you have..." 1Peter 3:15 , NIV. That scripture scared me! Could I out-argue an athiest? How could I explain the indescribable God of the universe and someone understand it? I no longer feel that pressure at all. God is capable of explaining Himself through His word found in the scriptures, the Holy Spirit, signs, wonders, and even in nature. I study His word not to out-argue or convince others but to know better the lover of my heart and soul.

The flight attendant talked about how challenging it was for her to explain being "born again." Everyone noticed how different she was, but it was hard to put into words WHY she was different. I recently read a scripture regarding that problem: "Jesus replied, "I tell you the truth unless you are born again, you cannot see the Kingdom of God. "What do you mean?" exclaimed Nicodemus. "How can an old man go back into his mother's womb and be born again?" John 3:4-5, NLT. Kind of confusing to explain the miracle of being given a new baby heart, spiritually speaking.

I totally got what she was saying. On my Holy Spirit adventures, trying to convince someone through reasoning with facts or even scriptures when they don't believe or care what the Bible says is like trying to use your fist and punch through a brick wall. If we are forcing it and not being led by the Holy Spirit, it's a waste of time. We can't reason with someone's mind if they already have it made up. No, the only way to "get to them" is to pray and ask the Holy Spirit to touch their hard heart...His love WILL crumble all their walls and allow an opening for his truth.

Holy Spirit adventure hack: I've found, if they let me simply pray for them, if they AGREE to it, then HE WILL reveal Himself to them because they agreed to the prayer... or if I can give them a hug as previous chapters have talked about. Prayer and love plant the seed. The agreement on their part is key. The Holy Spirit doesn't force or push. He's gentle and honors their choice to receive Him or not.

When we are God-led with agreement, it takes the pressure off of us. We don't get to take credit because it isn't through lofty words or persuasive speeches but through the power of the Holy Spirit. (1 Corinthians 2:1-5)

This particular flight attendant probably thought God sent me to her, but I know God sent her to me. On a day where I was really struggling and didn't have a smidgeon of love within me for the people around me.

God reminded me through my new friend that a hard day does go away. His mercies are new every day. She was God's answer to my prayer for strength and help. My day completely turned around, and I felt a touch from God through her encouraging faith.

"But let us who live in the light be clearheaded, protected by the armor of faith and love, and wearing as our helmet the confidence of our salvation...So encourage each other and build each other up, just as you are already doing."
1 Thessalonians 5:8, 11, NLT

Question

What do I need to flow in the Holy Spirit unhindered?

Circle one:

Encouragement

Hope

A word from God

Peace in my heart

Or write your own

....

CHAPTER 20

HOLY SPIRIT STOP SIGNS

My trip to LA started off really well. I had this super fun flight attendant as part of the crew. We'll call her Holly. She was British and had a cool accent. She knew I was a Christian, and I learned that she wasn't all in with Jesus but more seeking and leaning towards buddhism.

We made plans to go to Manhattan Beach the following day. Holly's husband called her while we were ubering to the beach. He would be driving through that area on his business trip and wanted to take her to lunch. I would now be flying solo. I thought the Holy Spirit kind of tricked me. I wouldn't normally go so far away from my layover hotel alone, but I knew it was God's plan to get me out and about for an adventure.

I asked the Holy Spirit to lead me, and I felt led to pray for my waitress, Stephanie. I wanted to ask her if she needed prayer, but I felt a Holy Spirit stop sign for the moment. I prayed for her while sitting alone at my table. After that prayer, I felt a release to share what I heard. I left a note for her about God working things in her favor and defending her. I sensed she might be going through a divorce or a breakup at the time. She really needed to know how loved she was during this time. Don't we all just need a little hope sometimes to keep going?

God's angels were guiding me by the shoulders the entire time I was in LA. That was a fun experience to be directed so intentionally by God. Los Angeles = City of Angels, indeed!

I would stop and feel a knowing. The Holy Spirit in me would hold up a red light, and I knew I needed to rest there for a moment. I would look in each direction, and then my feet would start moving, unbidden, as if the light had turned green. My spirit knew the map and timing even if I couldn't see it with my physical eyes. I saw the beach and wanted to go stick my toes in the sand but, again, I felt tugged in a different direction, so I stayed on the sidewalk in obedience and faith.

As I walked down the sidewalk, I saw another lady, and our paths were going to intersect. There were two sidewalks that met and shared about 3' of concrete. If we had continued walking, we would have collided with each other, but we both stopped. I didn't know why I chose to stop there (well, it was probably those angels), but I stood there trying to look normal. I was sitting at a Holy Spirit stop sign and waiting for the intersection to clear. I was listening, waiting, and watching for what, I didn't know. I felt like I was supposed to talk to her, but I didn't know what to say.

This kid on the beach nearby started wailing and throwing a really loud temper tantrum. The mother barked, "Stop that whining right now, or we are going home." She repeated herself a few times, but the kid kept wailing and throwing things. Still standing at this intersection, Diana and I both finally acknowledged each other. We gave each other that knowing "mom" nod and chuckled. Diana started the conversation as we watched the tantrum continue to unfold, "Stop whining, or we're going home." Diana said, "That's a good line. I need to use it on my teenage daughter."

I responded as if we were friends, "My son is about to go off to college, and I recently heard and tried out a great little line, but it was probably a little too late."

"What is it?"

"When he's disrespectful, I say, "You don't get to talk to me that way." Stops him in his tracks for some reason. Pretty genius. Wish I would have come up with it."

"I'll have to try that one too," she says as the mother yanks the kid's arm and drags him off the beach down the sidewalk making good on her promise to leave.

Diana had a really cool accent like my flight attendant friend. "Are you from the UK?"

"Uh no. Wrong continent. I'm Australian."

"Oh. Sorry."

We were chit-chatting for a bit. At some point, the thought must have crossed both of our minds that neither of us knew each other or why we were still standing there. I asked her about her children. She talked about her teenager, Jasmine.

I said, "I love that name. A flight attendant was showing me a book about flowers yesterday, and we talked specifically about the jasmine flower." (Remember, these are the things that the Holy Spirit uses to connect like a signpost along your adventures.)

She responded, "Funny thing. My much younger husband wants to have a child. We will name her Violet, another flower name. I've worked for my business for so many years, and I'm going to continue, but he wants to stay home if we have another baby."

Diana went on to tell me something so personal. She had ovarian cancer. She was healed but couldn't, and didn't really want to, have any more babies naturally. They were considering a surrogate.

I asked her what she did for a living. "I have a business to help people recover from heroin addiction." The name of her business reminded me of the Holy Spirit, and I told her so.

She had not mentioned Jesus or God in this conversation but what she said next was so cool. "The Holy Spirit exactly. I went away to the rainforest to seek God, and the Holy Spirit downloaded a method to heal people. My dad died of a heroin overdose when I was a child. I've used this Holy Spirit method, and it's healed many. The best part is it doesn't cost $80,000 for a rehab." I was so encouraged and excited by this time! I love God's ways of loving people. We discussed how God had us both "incognito" or "stealth" in our lines of work. She didn't advertise it in the recovery process unless they asked, but they got Jesus, God, and the Holy Spirit when they came to her program.

I said, "Well, I pray that God brings you Violet right on time. I believed that God would do it for her just like God had given Diana His pure method to heal and cure heroin addiction and cure her of ovarian cancer.

THE THINGS I LEARNED FROM THE HOLY SPIRIT:

1. **There are atmospheres over regions.**
   I shared this story with a friend after another recent Holy Spirit-led adventure to Los Angeles. "I just can't explain it, but I felt the presence of God so strongly while I was there." She was the person who reminded me, "Los Angeles means City of Angels." Oh yeah! It made sense. Whenever I go to LA, it has a "dream big" atmosphere over it, and I feel like anything is possible while I'm there. I also sense an air of entitlement there too. You will start to pick up on atmospheres as you go on adventures of your own.

2.   **Be led.**

To be led, we have to have our spiritual eyes and ears open. First, we have to have a soft heart and yield to the Spirit. We can't go on autopilot. The Holy Spirit leads us. He might change our direction or even throw up a stop sign. I initially thought this adventure was about Holly, the buddhist. I did have lots of conversations with Holly so maybe the faith I have in Christ planted a seed in her, but she wasn't the "mission." I was bummed when she got the call from her husband and a teensy bit scared about ubering back alone. We have to be flexible when plans change. I had to continue on in faith that I was exactly where God wanted me to be. I wasn't in control. I have to lay down my plans and trust Him. He led me to Stephanie and then to Diana.

3.   **Agreement in faith.**

We all have big dreams in our hearts. He led me to agree in faith with Diana on her daughter. We have things we carry from heaven that God has given us to share with each other. Faith. Wisdom. Revelation. We have access to these through our union with Christ, and we can share them.

"I also tell you this: If two of you agree here on earth concerning anything you ask, my Father in heaven will do it for you."
Matthew 18:19, NLT

Question

What do you need today to follow the signs of the Holy Spirit's direction?

Circle one:

An obedient heart

Eyes to see

Ears to hear

A soft heart

Sensitivity to the Holy Spirit

Or write your own

CHAPTER 21

WAITING ON THE
HOLY SPIRIT

I pull up to a cute little coffee shop in my area. Instead of getting out, I sit in my car. I scroll through social media, and a thought came to me. "Why am I in my car wasting gas with the a/c blowing full blast when I could be enjoying the free a/c in the coffee shop?" Still, I sat there, not knowing why. I sent some texts and read emails. All of a sudden, I felt myself turning the car off and getting out.

I see a woman who parked beside me getting out of her car and a fleeting thought came, "Maybe I was waiting for her?" I kept on walking and was a little miffed to find a long line to order.

I should have come in earlier instead of burning gas!

I didn't have any clear conscious thoughts from God, but I kept feeling a tug to turn around and talk to the lady I'd seen getting out of her car. See, sometimes we are waiting on God's booming voice to tell us to do something, but it's very rare that I hear His actual voice. Our Spirit knows the plan and is always leading us gently, but it takes faith and a willingness to be led. So I sense I'm to talk to her, but I'm trying to think of a way to strike up a conversation without being a "stranger danger" kind of person.

I see her hat, and it's got her initials on it. I'm a hat girl. "Cute hat," I say.

"Ahhh, thanks, but do you think the V looks like a J?"

"Yeah, my name's Jennifer, so I saw J, but I see now that it's a V." So now we have a connection made, but I still don't have much to say to this stranger. Thinking....hmmm. God, where are you going with this? I say, "Are you working on anything special today?"

"I'm a professor at ____ (big college), and I needed to get out of the house to focus. What about you?"

"Huh?" I said.

Distracted by her interesting outfit, I look at her. She is totally mismatched. She is wearing a man's red, yellow, and black plaid winter shirt in the summer, pinkish hat, ripped jean shorts, and white lace shirt? By the looks of her outfit, it was probably a rough morning. Maybe that's just her style, but she looked frazzled.

She repeated herself, "What about you? What do you do?"

"Oh, me? I'm a flight attendant, but I like to write, so I'm working on that today."

We talked about what I'm writing, and this segued into me telling her that I am about to take my youngest son to college. She shared she has a five and 7-year-old.

"I caught myself reminiscing on those days with my son. I know they are hard and have challenges, but I miss them."

She looked at me and said, "I need to remember that. We've had a really rough week. We flew your airline. My girls were both sick with a stomach bug and lost their lunch on the plane. I honestly couldn't wait to get out of the house to get away from it all. Thanks for the reminder that one day I will look back and cherish these days."

"Well, you're welcome." I ordered and said, "What are you having because I'm buying." (see, there was a reason she needed to be behind me in the line)

"Well, I was going to order a medium Chai Latte, but maybe I need to make it a small."

"Wow, that's probably the most expensive thing on the menu, but you're worth it!"

We both laughed.

"Thank you," she says.

"Consider it from your heavenly Father. He knows what you're going through, and He wanted to give you a little kiss today. It's all going to be all right, and He loves you so much."

"You know. I really, really needed this after the week I've had."

THREE THINGS I LEARNED THROUGH THAT INTERACTION ABOUT DIVINE APPOINTMENTS

1. **Timing is important.**
   He sets up divine appointments for us every day. It requires a sensitivity to His voice. If we are in a hurry or sleepwalking through life, we miss our "important to God appointments." What if I had rushed in to focus on my writing and gone with logic about wasting time, air conditioning, etc? Then, she wouldn't be behind me, and there would have been a misconnect, or what if I would have stewed about the wait when I came in? I would have been too frustrated to talk to her.

2. **Sometimes, we don't know what to say.**
   It doesn't have to be profound. The Holy Spirit is so gentle and kind. Just say something....anything...if you feel like you are on a Holy Spirit adventure, even if it's lame like "cute hat" to start the conversation. Our fear of rejection can keep us and others from making the connection. It might not have been a Holy Spirit adventure, and I would have found that out quickly if she was shut down or did not respond with an open heart.

3. **Be generous.**
   I'm counting my pennies right now. If I listened to my "never enough" voice, I would have been too cheap to "waste" gas or buy the drink. I planted a seed in her through our connection (she drank the latte/God's Koolaid—haha), so she received the gift from God, and who knows how that will play out with her attitude with her kiddos!

4. **Opportunities to love.**
   I probably miss a few opportunities every day because I'm doing my thing or frustrated with situations. I know God loves me still, but when I choose to follow his gentle lead, then I get to be part of the miraculous, and God's love for another. When we let His love flow through us, we experience it for ourselves.

"A new command I give you: Love one another. As I have loved you, so you MUST love one another."
Jn 13:34, NIV

Question

What do you need to wait in faith on the Holy Spirit?

Circle one:

A willing heart

A sign from God

Peace

More time with God to learn to be sensitive

Or write your own

....

CHAPTER 22

HOLY SPIRIT MAPS

A fellow flight attendant, we'll call her Layla, and I were on a 3-day trip. She was one of those fun flight attendants. She was not a control freak but, instead, very chill. God loves us, but it takes a special kind of person to be a flight attendant. Her enthusiasm for life and adventure was contagious. We were staying at a hotel in a not-so-great part of town. Layla and I weren't really interested in hanging outside of the liquor store or buying new tires at the tire store across the street, so we ubered to downtown Boston. We were planning on walking the Freedom Trail throughout the city. The trail is marked by a red brick line that runs down the middle of the sidewalk. If you follow the "red brick road," you get to walk the streets that hold landmarks of the great history of Boston.

We were dropped off in the middle of the city and were told, "The red brick road is very close. Just that way." The driver pointed between two buildings.

I held my hotel-provided map and flipped it around this way and that. I studied it, nodding and hmmmm-ing but not really knowing what I was doing. I think we've established the fact that I am GEOGRAPHICALLY CHALLENGED. One time, I told everyone I was going to Sweden when I was actually going to Switzerland. It's bad, guys. Turned out Layla was directionally impaired as well. We were trying to find that darn red brick line down the sidewalk. Everyone we asked said, "Right around the corner. You can't miss it. It's red!" they said in their cool, but snarky, Bostonian accents.

Instead of red bricks, we found a wharf on the water. I was like, "Woah, is Boston on the ocean?" To my surprise, it was! Layla said, "Why don't we let our spirit's lead us."

CREDIT CARDS

I was pretty pumped about going with the Holy Spirit flow. SO MANY DIVINE APPOINTMENTS happened on our few hours in Boston. Even though I was geographically challenged, I was learning more and more to trust the Holy Spirit map within me.

We were walking down the street, when Layla leaned over and picked something up off the ground, "I found a credit card." Upon further inspection, it was a doctor's credit card from the UK (that's basically Great Britain for those of you who don't know. I wasn't kidding about the geographically challenged thing.) Anyway, what are the odds of a credit card from the UK being under my British friend's feet in Boston? Layla was able to google him, call and leave his assistant a message so he wouldn't worry about it while "on holiday" (that's how the Brits say it). Who knew the Holy Spirit would help a brother or Brit out with his lost credit card?

We went with our gut (and ate with it) across that city. We were both in sync and agreed on our movements and turns. We did finally locate the elusive red brick road and saw some cool sights.

Holy Spirit confirmations came as we travelled in trust. We ended up at a local Boston favorite. The restaurant had just a handful of choices on its menu, but the line was out the door and down the block. The food was actually just okay, but the divine appointment while waiting in line was splendid. A dad and his son were in front of us. They grew up in Boston but now lived in San Diego. They were back for a short visit. Layla's husband was currently IN SAN DIEGO because they were considering moving there. The father/son duo were able to give her some neighborhoods to check out along with a lot of details on where NOT to live. Layla was being given direction through this divine appointment on her "next move," and what a sweet confirmation that San Diego was where she was being led!

TALKING TO A QUEEN

Next on the Holy Spirit's hit list: I met a young woman named Maria, who was a barista at a coffee shop that Layla and I both felt led to go into. She was wearing purple, and I felt like God said she was royalty like Queen Esther, so I told her. I asked her where she was from, and she, in turn, asked me. She said her friend went to Christ for the Nations in Dallas. I heard myself saying, "You'll be there next year!" Wait, where did that come from? Who am I to make that kind of statement, and what do I know?

She said, "My friend keeps asking, and I want to, but my husband isn't on board." I felt like God said that He would take care of that, and she wouldn't have to say a thing! It was so cool. I felt God's boldness to make such a statement. It was an honor to deliver this important message.

You may think, "Well, goodie for you because that stuff never happens for me."

It can happen for you. You only have to ask, listen and obey. It didn't happen for me until I asked and was willing to obey the Holy Spirit's nudges without having to have all the answers. I have no special skills other than obedience. I simply submit what I think and know, and ask God at every turning point to lead me. Things start to make sense in our life when we begin asking God for directions. Your adventures will not look exactly like mine, but there is a gentle nudge for our movements. The Holy Spirit is like a rider leading its' horse as we submit our day to His direction.

Many of us like to know what is coming so we can avoid pain or making a mistake, but the beauty and miracles come when we let go. We don't like moment-by-moment instructions of trying to find something we can't yet see or know. As you entrust your time to Him, your Spirit is reading the map. If you allow it, His map will lead you and guide you into an amazing life. He will surprise you with His love every step of the way.

"Trust in the Lord with all your heart and lean not on your own understanding; in all your ways, submit to him, and he will make your paths straight."
Proverbs 3:5-6, NIV

Question

What do you need to lay down your own life map and hear from God?

Circle one:

Sensitive ears

A prophetic word

Scheduling daily Bible time

A submitted heart

Trust

Or write your own

....

CHAPTER 23

GOD-INCIDENCES

I start noticing patterns when out of the five thousand flight attendants based at DFW, I end up seeing the same one more than once. My Holy Spirit antenna goes up to see what God is broadcasting, and I know it's probably a divine episode on God's heavenly reality show when I see someone multiple times. I know the angels are working to get us to a moment of connection to do what God wants done in our hearts.

There was definitely a pattern with one fellow flight attendant, Mariah, I kept running into. I went to a training class with her. She commuted home on one of my flights, then I was a passenger on one of her flights. I was the last one on the flight. With no seats left, I was sitting right next to her pretty face on the jumpseat. I felt a fondness in my heart for her like a daughter that I could not explain in the natural. My heart was filled with God's genuine love for her. I would say her relationship with God is pretty private, though, and maybe a little "to be determined" since she never mentioned it. I talked a lot about God. I know her sibling is in Bible school, but she never mentioned her own faith.

I hadn't pressed her or asked her anything about her personal faith. Our time together felt like God was opening her heart to me and building a level of trust. Slowly but surely, she was warming up to me. She confided in me her mom is self-centered, and she was the adult in the relationship.

As she worked her galley and served the passengers, I sat on the jumpseat and asked God what these little interactions were about. Did God have something to say to Mariah? My mind filled with an image. I saw Mariah lying on a beautiful beach in a pristine white bikini. Mariah was saying, "Do you see what God gave me? It's my new bathing suit. I love it! It fits me so perfectly."

Okay, STRANGE! First of all, you have to be really, really tan to pull off a white bathing suit, and she wasn't from the Caribbean. It's also hard to keep a white bathing suit clean on a beach!

I asked God, "So what does this picture mean?" I heard, "That is how I see her." She's pure, white, perfect, and spotless. She's my bride. I'm giving her this new bathing suit. It's hers. She doesn't have to do anything to earn it. I'm keeping it clean."

I asked if there was anything else He wanted to say. I heard a song begin playing in my mind called "Stay With Me." The lyrics that came to mind were, "Oh, won't you stay with me? 'Cause, you're all I need. I don't want you to leave, will you hold my hand?" I felt like these lyrics were Mariah's heart cry. She wasn't fearful or needy saying, "Please don't leave me, God!" No, she was strong, making a choice. "God, I want you to stay with me."

God was singing back to Mariah those lyrics too: "Stay with me!"

I hope you can feel God's heart towards this woman in what I write. He's so passionate and pleased with her. I know a white bikini and a secular song may not be how you might think God would speak, but God will speak to our hearts in the way only we can understand and appreciate at different stages in our lives. He will woo us from our desert.

Mariah may have looked for the love God was offering in men, again, not in a needy way, but, if I choose to let you have my body, then stay with me because another line of the song is "This ain't love, it's clear to see but won't you stay with me. And deep down, I know this never works. But you can lay with me, so it doesn't hurt..." One night stands offer faux love and leave us feeling empty, but we aren't alone, at least for that moment. It's not real love, though. The emptiness always comes back.

I completely related to her. I would have panic attacks at night and made a lot of bad choices because I was terrified to be alone. It's been hard to look to Him instead of trying to earn the love of men by being pretty enough.

All these sweet, crazy, and powerful thoughts were going through my mind, and I didn't know how to convey what I saw on the movie frame that rolled in my mind. When I first heard that secular song for her, I was offended. This vision and that song can't be from God. I was testing the spirit from which it came, but I felt a peace about it in my heart. God would meet her where she was and speak to her in a language she would understand. Mariah shared with me that she grew up in a religious home, but then her parents got divorced. I knew God would create the opportunity to share if it was Him, so I put it to the side for the moment and just prayed.

After Mariah finished her service, she sat down, and we chatted. She talked about what was going on in her life. She's a no-nonsense, strong girl and so brave. I gave her some advice about confronting a self-focused person in her life. Mariah tends to be pretty direct and she wanted to be gentle this time.

I remarked on how God had brought us together several times (not a coincidence but a God-incidence). I asked permission to share what I felt like I heard from God for her. She consented. I shared the bathing suit vision and the lyrics of the song. She also confirmed she was feeling very lonely in this job. I asked her if I could pray for her. In the prayer, I asked God to be real to Mariah. To hold her as she fell asleep and that she would feel His nearness. That He would indeed stay with her.

Her tears were so profuse that they covered my arms like little rivers. Nothing I said was profound, but God's love is like that. It touches the lonely places of our hearts so deeply that our hard hearts are broken into a thousand pieces. During these times, the hurt in our hearts is released to Him. His love gives us a new and pure start, a thousand times over if needed. He's putting the pieces of our broken heart back together, little by little. I love how God loves us.

"But then I will win her back once again. I will lead her into the desert and speak tenderly to her there."
Hosea 2:14, NLT

Question

What do you need to reach those you know aren't living the highest
and best plan for their lives? Do people's life choices offend us? Do
we think God wants to reach those who seem far from Him? Journal
about it and ask God what He thinks.

Circle one:

Patience

Release from judgment

Love for the lost

Jesus glasses

Or write your own

....

CHAPTER 24

LOADED QUESTIONS

"Well, I'm not going to say it's okay, when it's not okay! Sometimes, "they" are trying to trap you with questions like that. That's why I didn't answer. Justin asked us a loaded question, and the answer is NO, I'm not going to condone sin!" That was from Cheryl, a flight attendant. I was working side-by-side with her on a three-day trip.

The night before this conversation, our crew of flight attendants decided to try the local cuisine. Our interesting meals were placed before us with a flourish. I looked suspiciously at it since my husband told me the island was overrun with lizards. My husband snickered when he said they tried to sneak the lizard in local dishes as a mystery meat. Probably best to pray for a meal like that.

Cheryl, the loaded-question lady, was already digging in, and Justin, our co-worker, was sipping on his Mojito. I didn't know, at that time, if either of them were Christians. I asked a little hesitantly, "Would you guys mind if I pray? If it bothers you, then I'll say mine privately. It's really no problem, and I'm sorry if this is putting you on the spot."

Justin, who has a boyfriend from New York, said, "Sure. Do it. Pray." Justin went on to say that his mom always prayed before meals too. Cheryl, a piece of shrimp hanging out of her mouth, assented with a nod as well. I prayed some specific things for each of them. For Justin, I prayed that he would see God clearly. For Cheryl, I asked that she would feel how special she was to God...that He would comfort her and she was His chosen bride. Of course, I remembered to bless the fresh lizard.

After the prayer, Cheryl shared she was a former Church of Christ-er and now went to a non-denominational church. I kind of figured there was a story behind that comment.

Then came the loaded question from Justin that so upset Cheryl: "So you say you're Christians. I'm curious, how do you feel about equality of marriage and all that?"

Cheryl stayed quiet. A story came to mind from my past. I was a brand new baby Christian. I had a meeting with a same-sex couple who were realtors. They were partners in business and in life. On my way to meet them for lunch, I told God (not really expecting an answer) "God, Jennifer really likes both of these ladies, but If YOU want me to tell them the truth that what they are doing is wrong (speaking of their same-sex relationship) then I WILL!" I had my own similar experience like this when I was younger, so was I really in a place to talk about wrong or right to anyone? Still, I had been reading the Bible, and it seemed SO CLEAR: wrong versus right. I was fairly surprised when God responded to me and said, "Jennifer, this is none of your business. I didn't call you to this meeting to judge them I called you to love. If you can't love these women, then at least be kind to them for me."

I was confused and thinking maybe the voice in my head wasn't Him... but He made it clear. Crystal clear, in fact...about how He felt about me telling them how wrong they were. I argued with the voice, "But what if they go to hell because I didn't tell them?" God doesn't take it kindly when I talk about his kids and push my own agenda when He has other plans for that specific conversation.

I felt righteous anger in the force of His response to me. Like a lion roaring, He was fierce. "Don't you dare touch my daughters' hearts. You'll have to get through me first." As a mother, I understood His protective stance. If I need to deal with my kiddos on something, then that is a PRIVATE matter between ME and THEM. It would be like me spanking someone else's child without authority. I would be fighting against God Himself if I proceeded. (Am I saying you shouldn't speak the truth in love? No. Absolutely not. However, we have to be connected to the Holy Spirit in order to know WHAT to say and WHEN to say it. I did talk to one of the women later during their break up AFTER she knew I loved her and our relationship was established.)

Justin listened intently to my story about my conversation with the realtors. I didn't even leave out the part about "if you want me to tell them the truth." Justin could have been offended. I did not answer his question directly. Instead, Justin shared about his mom's battle with cancer and her supernatural testimony of meeting God. It was powerful. She was in a room sick from cancer, and a light began shining brighter and brighter on her. His mom saw an image of herself bent over with the devil jumping on her back. She had not been a Christian before that encounter, but she had given her life completely to God. Justin's mom went to church "all the time" now. He wasn't sure about Jesus, and, at this point in his life, he shared, "Currently, I'm not a Christian." I believe Justin's momma had been praying for her sweet boy, and God sent me to be salt and light.

As the conversation went on, Justin shared more about himself. He talked about a dark period of his life not that long ago. He had gone to outpatient therapy for alcoholism and "other stuff." He had battled deep depression to the point of giving up. He was so tired of suffering.

I learned on this Holy Spirit adventure that we must be in moment-by-moment communication with Him to release the right word at the right time. To be fruitful in the Spirit, we have to double-check that our words are from God by at least ASKING God how He feels before we speak! We don't know the depths of others' suffering. God will protect hurting hearts from people like ME (remember with the realtors?). Only God knows how much Justin has been through and what needed to be said at that moment.

A girl asked me last week, "Should I live with my boyfriend?" I wanted to say, "NO! It's not wise!" The guy she is dating is still "in process," for sure. I asked the Holy Spirit before I spoke and went into fearful mommy mode. I heard, "She already knows her answer, so ask her." I asked if she'd heard anything from God on it. She said, "Yes, but I still don't know." We prayed, and I prayed for her. She texted me this week that she knew it wasn't a good idea, and she was making changes to rectify the situation. God has the greatest wisdom, even if it's just asking questions. His answers to my own questions on how to handle situations surprise me.

We can't affirm other people's sins. The Bible is the foundation of truth. It does.not.change.ever. but our words, what to share and when, are to be led by the Holy Spirit. He knows. I have had discussions where I confronted sin in no uncertain terms. These conversations were with people I was in relationship with and my heart was full of love and a desire for restoration for them with Jesus. Jesus didn't bring the hammer down with the the prostitutes or the woman at the well. Jesus only said what He heard the Father saying. He put himself between the woman caught in the act of adultery. Then, He restored her to the truth privately. He saved his harshest words for the religious.

"The LORD appeared to him from afar, saying, "I have loved you with an everlasting love;
Therefore, I have drawn you with lovingkindness."
Jeremiah 31:3, NASB 1995

"Or do you have no regard for the wealth of His kindness and tolerance and patience
[in withholding His wrath]? Are you [actually] unaware or ignorant [of the fact] that
God's kindness leads you to repentance [that is, to change your inner self, your old way of
thinking—seek His purpose for your life]?"
Romans 2:4, AMP

Question

Do you avoid conversations like I had with Justin? If so, why?

What do you need from the Holy Spirit to have the uncomfortable conversations?

Circle one:

Love in my heart

The ability to connect with the Holy Spirit

A listening ear

God's heart

Or write your own

....

CHAPTER 25

CHERYL

Remember Cheryl from the previous chapter? Don't worry, I haven't forgotten about her either. I learned a valuable lesson from the Holy Spirit through my interactions with her. The following morning, after our dinner with Justin, Cheryl vented to me in the front galley. She didn't like Justin's loaded question. Cheryl wanted to explain her silence at his question on gay marriage. God's word is clear on gay marriage, and we both knew it. I agreed with her about being silent though. "You are right. It is sometimes wise to be silent if we don't have love in our heart towards the person we are speaking with."

Cheryl said, "Well, you know. Love the sinner. Hate the sin." That comment felt off to me in that moment. I felt gossipy talking about Justin when he was in the back of the plane. I may have answered too strongly in my tone when I said, "Justin's sin is really none of my business. Jesus said, "A new commandment I give to you: "Love your neighbor as yourself," right? How do I want to be treated by others? I want to be treated gently and with love even in the midst of my sin. I want restoration with truth AND kindness." I continued, "I asked the Holy Spirit, and I hope to God He led me in what I said to Justin."

It was a sharp reply. I didn't expect Cheryl to confide in me at that moment. My heart broke for her as she shared she had been cheated on too many times to count by her husband, a full-time pastor. After many long years of marriage with a newborn baby, he left her for an eighteen-year-old girl. He met the girl in the youth ministry and had been sleeping with her for two years. Cheryl looked off and her voice choked up as she said, "He kept saying he would stop, but he never did." She had been given counsel by the church to forgive him. Cheryl chose to follow that advice to keep her family together, but it all still fell apart. Her husband's choices had devastated her and destroyed her family (her words), so she would never say another's sin was okay again.

There it was. Cheryl had deep, life-altering pain associated with another person's sin. Her comment about being unable to condone sin made complete sense now.

I felt such compassion for her as she shared her story, eyes darting to make sure no one walked up to hear her shame. She had loved her husband. She suffered and was willing to die for her marriage, but she was not given a voice or a choice. The person she was protecting from stones put a knife in her back. He proved through his actions that he cared more for himself and his desires than he did her or their family. "He threw us away," she said angrily during one part of her story.

It's a very fine line when dealing with other people's choices that affect me personally and directly. Justin hadn't cheated on her or sinned against her. She made a "never again" vow which we can all fall prey to. This vow had her in bitter bondage. She could not see Justin with eyes of love. Her glasses for life were clouded with unforgiveness. Her emotions were fear-based, and her heart had not healed though it had been twelve years since it happened. Don't we all have areas of brokenness that stir up anger within our own hearts?

I remember during a very difficult season with someone else's abuse, I cried out to God, "I want to let go, but I can't. I feel like if I let go then it makes it right, and it wasn't right!" After weeks of processing, I finally wrote a letter releasing this person into God's hand. The person called me the next week and said, "God said I will have no peace until I make things right with you." This person wasn't even walking the life of a Christian when I received this call. I wanted justice in my time and in my way, in order to be able to forgive, release and bless them. It doesn't always happen so quickly. I have other injustices I'm still waiting on God to make right, but I have peace in my heart. I forgive every day until I receive His peace. God wants us to put it in his capable hands to bring us true justice in His perfect timing.

I'm thankful for Justin's loaded question. Through the process, Cheryl might be able to gain a new perspective from God if she allows it. It's very liberating NOT to be responsible for other's choices. It frees us up to love them and see beyond the speck of dust in their eye. My prayer for her at the meal was that she would feel comforted. Even if her husband 'threw her away,' God chose her. She was very special to Him. The prayer over the meal in the last chapter was for her. I love how the Holy Spirit knew her heart.

"Be kind and compassionate to one another, forgiving each other, just as in Christ God forgave you."
Ephesians 4:32, NIV

"And we know that in all things God works for the good of those who love him, who have been called according to his purpose."
Romans 8:28, NIV

"He who was seated on the throne said, "I am making everything new!" Then he said, "Write this down, for these words are trustworthy and true."
Revelation 21:5, NIV

Question

Have you been harmed by someone else's sin? I know I have. I lived so much of my life in pain and unforgiveness. Are you ready to release that to Jesus? Journal about it.

What do I need from the Holy Spirit to forgive?

Circle one:

A willing heart

To recognize my own sin

God's help

Putting it on the altar of God's grace

Or write your own

....

CHAPTER 26

EMPATHY

I was on the fourth day of waking up at 3 a.m. It was so early, the coffee shops hadn't even opened their eyes yet. The crew was onboard long before the sun was scheduled to peek over the horizon. A jumpseater headed back in our direction to catch a ride with us. Since she was on the jumpseat, this meant that every single seat on the airplane was taken. Full boat. I try to be kind to jumpseaters.

This girl was something else, though. "Porcupine Patty" was fairly persnickety from the time she got onboard. The other flight attendants and I were lamenting about how early it was and how the lack of coffee was affecting our brain cells. She inserted herself into the conversation and reminded us we were on west coast time, so it meant it was only 5 a.m. our time. I'm sorry, did anyone ask you for your two cents, PATTY? My watch says THREE, not FIVE. I know. Not very "Christianly" thoughts, but it was 3 a.m., excuse me, 5 a.m. I wasn't in the mood. Deep breaths, Jennifer, deep breaths.

I responded, "Well, Patty, we had to get up at 3 a.m. for the last three days."

She gave me a "Suck it up, buttercup" look.

I could have thrown out something really witty like, "This is an A to B conversation, so C your way out of it." But that one's really lame, and I couldn't think of anything else. I know you guys never get into the flesh or lose your Jesus like me.

I sighed. I closed my eyes and prayed, "God, only you know how hard this four-day trip has been on me with thirteen-hour+ days. It's easy to have a lack of empathy when it's NOT YOU doing the suffering. Lord, I give Patty and her petty comments to you because I don't want to talk to her anymore. I know you love her, though."

After the prayer, I felt the grace start to flow again. When I was done setting up, I said, "Can I get you a bottled water, Patty?"

Her reply, "You're a little late. The flight attendant up front already got me one."

Oh, no, she didn't. I turned around and breathed more deep breaths. A simple "No, thank you" would have sufficed. God, I'm done. It's too early to deal with snarky and unhappy flight attendants. I prayed another prayer because I'd already lost my Jesus again. I asked God to give her an attitude adjustment and decided it was best to completely ignore this person. I had zero love in my heart for Patty. I prayed again, "Jesus, help me love her like you do!"

It was a fairly long flight, and wasn't I so lucky that Patty was sitting right next to me on my jumpseat? I guess God convicted Patty because she lost the attitude. Prayer works! As we sat next to each other, she opened up about how she was going to visit her mom who was having surgery the following day. I asked for her mom's name and offered to pray.

"It's no big deal," Patty says.

"Oh, what's she having done?"

"Heart surgery."

"Um, Patty, I would say that's a pretty big deal."

"Yeah."

Patty put her hand on her head. I asked, "You okay?"

She said, "I get migraines."

I said, "I'm so sorry. It's the worst to fly with a migraine. Everything is exaggerated in the air. Can I get you an Advil or anything else?"

"Thank you. I think I'm okay for now." Her face softened.

She went on to share a lot about her life. Another "Jumpseat Confession." She talked about losing her first husband suddenly, more about her Mom's heart surgery and then her debilitating headaches. Patty said, "I never complain, but this is a real thing. Over the years, flying has done a number on my body, so I finally went to the doctor to be able to avoid flying when I have a migraine. I've always judged people who went on family leave for illnesses as "fakers," but now I understand."

I talked to her about how a couple of days after a stressful situation, I would get a bad headache. I felt like God told me it was me turning the stress and taking it out on myself. Anxiety would come after the stressful situation with a mental bombardment of negative thoughts saying, "You could have done it differently...

Why did that have to happen...God isn't with me...Bad things always happen to me." This type of self talk was really self-hatred.

I felt like I got this download from God when Patty talked about her mom and minimized something as serious as heart surgery. Patty's mom never showed her an ounce of compassion because she wanted her to be strong. Patty wasn't being snarky. She was modeling what she knew. I totally recognized the attitude.

My daughter was twelve when I had an encounter with God that changed every single thing about my life. Pre-Jesus, I had a "put your big girl panties on and deal with it" attitude like Patty. I realized I had, in trying to teach my own daughter to be strong, withheld showing her softness. Once I "woke up" and had an encounter with God, I apologized to my daughter, "In my attempt to grow you into a self-sufficient and strong woman, I missed out on showing you love. I'm so sorry. Will you please forgive me?"

She smiled her teenage brace-face smile and said, "You're perfect, Mom, but, of course, I forgive you."

"You're so sweet, Monica, but how can I make this right?" She thought for a moment and said, "I like hugs."

We hugged for the first time in a long time and for what felt like an hour. I cried my eyes out for what I had missed, for what she had lacked, and for the gratefulness that there was still lots of time left to hug.

TAKEAWAYS FROM MY TIME WITH PATTY

1.   **We can have empathy without enabling bad behavior.**
     How could Patty have empathy for my exhaustion when she had never received it for herself? I believe, through our interaction, I modeled how to be compassionate and empathetic—at least, I hope I did because there were those times I wanted to throw her off the airplane.

2.   **Pray instead of fighting fire with fire.**
     Sometimes this involves taking moments for deep breaths and time outs for prayer.

"Cast all your anxiety on him because He cares for you."
1 Peter 5:7, NIV

Question

How do you respond to difficult people? What do you need from the
Holy Spirit to remain in His love? Take time to journal about it.

Circle one:

Peace in my heart

Forgiveness for myself

Empathy

Compassion

Love

Or write your own

....

CHAPTER 27

DIFFERENT

I was headed to Atlanta. As usual, my flight was set up by the Man upstairs. Blake was a jumpseater strategically placed RIGHT next to me. I'm convinced that jumpseats were actually made for elves and Blake was not an elf in any way. He was a big old burly boy. He looked like the guy on the Brawny paper towel ads. I teetered on the edge of our shared seat.

Most guys I fly with, er um, like guys. When I started flying, I was plotting how I might get them into a church. I realized very quickly they had been more wounded by people who sat in pews than anyone else. It's a really sad fact. I have found that many people God sends me to have been hurt by the church.

Blake was no different. He believed in the "universe" and was "spiritual" but had shunned religion. He told me about some of his experiences at church. A guy refused to shake his hand because he found out he was gay. "Everyone who is religious that I meet seems to make it their personal mission to get me to stop sinning because I am gay." We had a really nice conversation where I was able to share some of my testimonies of God on the airplane. He said the conversation was refreshing. "I can't have these kinds of conversations with religious people because they want to judge me and call me a sinner. I can't tell you how many people have called me ugly names, spat at me. I've got scars all over my body from the wounds. Literal scars." He almost whispered those last words. It broke my heart to see this man so hurt by Christians. I can see it from both sides: Christians don't want to stamp approval on something against God's word, but still, Blake deserved kindness and tenderness not being spit on! What if the man who refused to shake his hand had given him a father's hug and offered to walk with him in life? What if he offered to pray for him rather than keeping his hand in his pocket?

The thing that struck me about Blake was his willingness to understand why Christians were so against gay marriage. He said Christians were really defensive and hadn't been able to give him a good answer. Blake said he was befuddled, and the only reason he could come up with was their judgmental attitude. "Why are you Christians so offended if I have the same rights as you have? How does it hurt you in any way?"

I had been in a holding pattern waiting to hear from God in our conversation. I definitely have thoughts to share on gay marriage. Same sex commitments could be called partnerships or something else but leave God's covenant, called marriage, out of it. When I ask God how I should answer questions that, in my mind, have a black and white answers, many times, He doesn't really answer the question the way I think He will.

A dear friend who has devoted her life to helping people who are married stay that way was gutted when the laws changed to allow gay marriage...as in tears for days...can't get off the couch...devastated. She's not a hater either. She's just sad.

Blake was so earnest in his desire to understand why Christians were against gay marriage. I asked the Holy Spirit what to say. My eyes fell on his work lanyard. I said it out loud, "What if someone tried to change the name of our airline that you proudly hang around your neck to generic airlines. Anyone can work here. How would you feel?" He was an "old-timer" with our company. I continued, "Would you feel that was right? Would you be angry? Upset at all?"

Blake opened his mouth to say something and closed it. He finally said, "I don't know. I don't think that's the same thing, but I don't know. I'll have to think about it."

I asked the Holy Spirit for more, but I didn't hear anything else. I let the Holy Spirit do what only He can do: Bring conviction, truth, and plant the seed.

I could tell Blake was a compassionate person who truly wanted to see the situation and understand it. I prayed God would continue to speak to Blake's heart on the subject.

Blake and I parted with a hug and mutual respect for each other.

Did I convert Blake at that moment? No. It would have felt really good to debate him on the Bible and win him over, but that's not what God led me to do. So many times, we speak on principle and not on a word from the Holy Spirit. I've spoken so many times without asking for God's words. I don't always have the maturity of obedience to ask the Holy Spirit, wait and hear from the Lord. Jesus was really good about sometimes not answering the Pharisees' questions directly while being really kind to sinners who were open to losing their spiritual blindness.

"Then you will know the truth, and the truth will set you free."
John 8:32, NIV

"For the Holy Spirit will teach you at that time what needs to be said."
Luke 12:12, NLT

Question

Do you struggle when people ask you hard questions?
The Holy Spirit can help!

What do you need to have Spirit-led conversations?

Circle one:

Revelation

Knowledge

Fear of the Lord

Awakening

A listening ear

Or write your own

....

CHAPTER 28

SUNSHINE GIRL

I was in Tulsa, and I was thrilled. I was close to my son's college town. I called him to see if he had time for lunch, but he declined. He said it was his busy day. I was a little sad, thinking God had given me this "surprise" reserve trip to Tulsa to see him. I wanted to call my son back and say, "I know you are going to eat lunch, so we can figure this out," but that would be playing wounded mommy, and honestly, God is working on me with that.

I decided to go to my favorite place to write called Foolish Things. It's a really cool hipster spot with good food. God sometimes sits my divine appointments right in front of me, so I looked up. A tatted-up girl with a pretty low-cut shirt was sitting directly across from me. I've learned on my adventures with the Holy Spirit, that God doesn't have a type. He just loves His kids. Even Jesus might have a tat. "On his robe and on his thigh, he has this name written: King of kings and Lord of lords." Revelation 19:16

I started to pray for this young woman under my breath. I asked God if He wanted to say something. I heard nothing but continued to silently pray for her. I asked God to allow her to feel His presence and know His love. Have you ever met someone that had an old boyfriend's unwanted name tattooed on them? I felt like God was coming in through my prayers and covering her old life and loves. Getting "inked" can be painful, but little by little, she would be marked with the love of her Heavenly Father. Instead of her snake tattoos, Jesus was covering her with a garden of flowers.

The Holy Spirit was showing me this in real-time in my mind. The prayers prayed were making little splashes of paint on her heart. The beginning of a new masterpiece covering up some of her wounds.

"Anything else, God?" I still heard nothing, and at that moment, she got up and left. "God, did I miss an opportunity?" I heard nothing.

Immediately, an adorable little sweetheart of a girl came and sat in tatted girl's seat. Once again, God's angels brought the next object of his affection to sit across from me. I felt like God's tattoo artist with my own chair. Prayer was God's ink. Next up!

She was such a sunshine girl, but I didn't see any tattoos. Her smile radiated and glowed. The glory of the Lord was upon her. I could feel it. Her face was open, but I was at a loss on how to get the ball rolling if I was, indeed, supposed to speak to her. I had to go to the bathroom, so a lightbulb went off. "Hey, can you watch my computer?"

"Sure. No problem," she replied with a smile.

When I came back, I still didn't have some divine epiphany or prophetic word, so I asked her if she was having a good day.

"Yeah. It's great."

"Oh, good!" Conversation over.

She waited a few seconds and then said, "Other than I have a biology test in a few hours, and I can't believe it, but I haven't prepared for it at all. You wouldn't believe all of the problems of getting my book. It got lost in the mail. They wouldn't refund my money, so I had to wait to have enough money to order a new one. I seriously can't believe I'm in this situation. I might fail." The smile left her face, and she looked overwhelmed. She pursed her lips together and blew out as she flipped through the book. I guess her day wasn't so great after all...

"Well, I love to pray. Would you like me to pray for you?"

"Sure."

I prayed for her to retain information and for God to help her succeed and to have a fresh start without feeling like she was behind.

She said, "Thanks," and I thought the conversation was over.

But just to confirm, I asked God, "Anything else?" I saw a picture of her in my mind sitting next to a window in a sunlit room. She was singing, and her face was reflecting the sun. It was so beautiful.

I looked over at her, wondering if I should share. She still had a look of consternation on her face as she stared at her biology book.

Nope, God, sorry, I am not going to interrupt her again from her last-minute study time, and I had already used the "watch my computer" excuse.

I looked at my computer screen and an email notification popped up, and the subject line said, "SINGING..." Oddly enough, the email had nothing to do with singing! LOL, but I knew it was a confirmation from God that I was to share.

So, tentatively, I interrupted her studying. "Hey, I know this is a strange question but do you play an instrument or sing?" I was expecting her to say no, and then I don't know what I would have said. It probably would have been, "No, yeah, I didn't think so. Me neither." Then, I would have run out of the coffee shop. She looked a little shocked, though, and said, "Yes! Why?" I LOVE these bread crumbs sprinkled on our path by God. They let us know we are on the right track and to keep going.

"Well, I know this may sound funny, but I felt like God showed me a picture of you sitting at a window singing, and the sun came and shone on your face. You are truly glorious when you sing, and I feel like you will have peace when you sing."

"I can't believe you just asked me if I sing!" She shared that her sister had taken guitar lessons and just couldn't get the hang of it. However, she had picked up the guitar as a little girl and taught herself to play.

It was a simple word, but she said, "I am texting my sister what you said. I told her that I had been struggling lately, and she randomly JUST asked me if I ever play the guitar anymore, because I seemed so happy when I do it. I haven't had time. I just can't handle all this anxiety or stress about money and school. My mind won't stop worrying. I've tried to stop it. I've been on my own for a long time, and I've had a black cloud over me all day. Actually, this whole week. Well, it's probably been hanging around all year."

I love how God broke through her dark clouds with his warm and sunny love. First with the prayer, then with a word that He knew would touch her heart.

WHAT I LEARNED

1.   **Discernment and wisdom are needed on Holy Spirit adventures.**
      We need the wisdom to know when to boldly speak and when to be. silent like with the tatted girl. We can only get this by asking the Holy Spirit.

2.   **We have to be willing to look foolish or be wrong.**
      I seriously didn't know what she would say about singing, which scared me. She had been struggling for a year! God will allow the sunshine in our hearts to break through another's dark clouds if we will step out in faith. God could give you the key to someone else's chains bringing freedom and breakthrough. Journal about what's keeping you from speaking what you hear from the Holy Spirit.

"Arise, shine, for your light has come, and the glory of the LORD rises upon you. See, darkness covers the earth, and thick darkness is over the peoples, but the LORD rises upon you, and his glory appears over you."
Isaiah 60:1-2, NIV

Question

What do you need from God to share what you see and hear from the Holy Spirit?

Circle one:

Confirmations

Peace

No shame

Word of knowledge

Gift of prophecy

Or write your own

....

CHAPTER 29

GIFTS OF THE HOLY SPIRIT

My daughter and I had plans for a Saturday morning brunch date. We both thought God might be sending us on one of His special missions to some strangers who needed to be encouraged. We considered how we might be able to plant seeds of His love in hearts. The night before our brunch, I hammered some metal necklaces with words that said different things like "Brave" and "Joy." I also brought a few cards with us to write on to deliver messages if the Holy Spirit led.

We prayed about where to go. My husband thought we should go to a local breakfast place. It was the weekend before Christmas, and the cafe was always so crowded. We asked the Holy Spirit, and both of us felt led to go there. Maybe God would put us right at the front of the line since we were on HIS special mission, but, no, that didn't happen. We waited for thirty minutes for our table.

We were finally seated. Monica immediately said she felt like we needed to write a card for the young twenty-something couple at the table next to ours. Monica sensed God saying they were a "power couple." They were like peanut butter and jelly or ice with tea. They were both very different, but were made to complement each other. They were a team. She wrote it all down. I also felt like God said the young lady would have two kids, and she should not listen to any bad reports because it would all be fine! I prayed, and God said not to write that part down, so I kept mum on the subject of her being a mom. I was so proud of my daughter when she boldly went to give them the card. It takes a lot of courage to walk up to strangers with a "word from God."

I watched on and asked God why He would tell me about her two babies but not allow me to deliver such a message. I prayed for her and the two little ones that would one day be part of their team and felt peace.

I wasn't surprised when our waitress just so happened to be a girl I prayed for when she was pregnant at a different restaurant five years earlier. ONLY God! So a necklace went to her... along with a big Christmas tip from Jesus. Being the Holy Spirit's messenger on an adventure is SO fun!

The young couple we gave the card to came over as they were leaving. They asked where we went to church. They happened to go to our church, but it was a big one, so we'd never met. They explained how God brought them to the busy cafe. They tried to go to other less crowded places because they had too much to do that day. His mom was making breakfast, and he never passed up a meal, but they both still wanted to go to this specific place. It didn't make sense to them, but NOW IT DID!

During this conversation, God said I could FINALLY tell her about the two babies He had in the works for her. I shared what God told me. If she was ever afraid, not to worry. All would be okay.

She said, "You have no idea, but that is my greatest fear and has been all my life. I am so afraid of being pregnant and giving birth!"

WOW! God is good. He planted a seed of peace in her heart through this word for when the time was right! We found out later this young couple paid for our breakfast. God blesses us, and we get to bless others on these Holy Spirit-led adventures.

We were about to leave, and I had one necklace left. I felt like one of the necklaces and cards were for a single older lady who had lost someone dear to them. They would be alone this Christmas, but I didn't see anyone who fit that description. We were about to leave when an older lady sat down all by her lonesome at the table next to us!

We felt the hand of God that Christmas week. God sends us to bring good news and encourage others. He commands us to GO! To reach those He loves. We teach our kids to stay safe, but God says even though we may be lambs among wolves, He will protect us.

Jesus said:

"During my time here, I protected them by the power of the name you gave me. I guarded them so that not one was lost...I'm not asking you to take them out of the world, but to keep them safe from the evil one."
John 17:12,15, NLT

He will protect you as you love on His peeps! The people around you are not strangers to their Father in heaven. He knows them each by name. He knows the number of babies He will entrust to them. He knows the hairs on their head, and not one little sparrow falls without Him knowing and caring about it. They are His children who He loves dearly and wants to speak to THROUGH YOU!

"And may you have the power to understand, as all God's people should, how wide, how long, how high, and how deep his love is. May you experience the love of Christ, though it is too great to understand fully. Then you will be made complete with all the fullness of life and power that comes from God."
Ephesians 3:18-19, NLT

What's stopping you from allowing God to share this amazing love through you? You might think, "I don't even know where to start. HOW would I do this?" It's easy! Ask Him, and God will create the opportunity and bring the people to YOU just like He did for us!

You might not be crafty enough to hammer a necklace or have the supplies. You might be really shy. What if you bought someone's meal like the couple did for us with a little note including your favorite scripture on it? Something so simple can show and flow His love through you! Will you do it? All it takes is a willing heart! Do one simple act of love for a stranger today.

"The Lord... sent them two by two...He told them, 'The harvest is plentiful, but the workers are few...Go! I am sending you out like lambs among wolves.'"
Luke 10:1-3, NIV

Question

What do you need to step out in faith and bless another?

Circle one:

Holy Spirit boldness

A touch from God

Open heart

Belief

Or write your own

....

CHAPTER 30

MOM-ING

A friend and I met for lunch. We both felt like the Holy Spirit was leading us to Chick-fil-a. We thought God might have a divine appointment for us there. We also knew they had fries and ice cream. Ha.

A twenty-five-ish-year-old guy was behind the counter and took our order. I remarked to my friend how much he looked like her teenage son with his dimples, and she said, "I love dimples." The guy kind of blushed, and I said quickly, "I promise we aren't flirting, we are mom-ing. Bless you." That ended up being prophetic.

We sat in the corner chatting. My friend got up quickly, "I'll be right back." There was this young college-aged guy about to walk out of the restaurant. She asked him if he had a minute. The guy said, "Well, I'm on my way to school and, to be honest, I'm a little hung over." To hear her tell this was HILARIOUS because she said, "I just skipped on past that hangover part." I don't think she's ever been drunk in her life. I laughed when she said, "I told him I could make it quick." She told him no matter how his parents acted, if he could just honor them, God would give him a great blessing. He received it and thanked her.

She asked him if she could give him a hug, and he said, "Yes!"

So, that weekend, I was working alongside a young flight attendant. She shared about her life. "My only religion is veganism," she said. We talked about being a democrat and/or liberal. She was adorable and lovely really, even though we lived polar opposite lives. I realized I had flown with her before. She said, "Oh, yeah, that was when I was living with Tyler in Dallas, but now I am living with Brian in San Antonio." She reminded me so much of myself in my younger years (other than the vegan part).

During our time together, she was hardcore trying to convert me to "veganism," which was HILARIOUS. She was saying all this while I was mmm-mmming over my bacon, egg, and cheese biscuit. I explained, through bites, that my boys were big-time hunters. We had a freezer full of game. I loved MEAT way too much to be a vegan. I think we all have to listen to our bodies and do what's best for us as individuals though. She was fine with that and wasn't repulsed by my carn(ivor)ality.

We talked about our significant others. I don't know how we got on the subject, but we started talking about "love languages." (You might have to google it if that's a new term for you.) She made a pretty big deal about how her number one love language was physical touch. She said, "There's just something about physical touch that makes me feel loved." I didn't even realize I was saying it, but I said, "Could I give you a hug?" She said, "I would love that." When we hugged, I prayed silently that God would be so close to her and hug her whenever she needed it most. She didn't let go for a bit.

The hungover guy at Chick-fil-a. His heart was broken. He was chasing peace. Maybe he was hurt from his mom and dad's choices. Maybe from his own, but honestly, it doesn't matter. My friend who hugged him is an amazing mom. Spiritually, I think she heard his heart cry and a longing for healing. He NEEDED that hug in his heart to get past his pain. He couldn't do it alone. She mom-ed him with that hug and brought comfort and peace through it. A hug can forever change one's trajectory and can change their whole life's direction.

To have a Holy Spirit adventure, we don't need some epiphany or glorious word from God or fantastic bit of wisdom to solve their problems. Those types of encouragements are awesome, but all we need are two arms and a willing heart. Hugs heal! Especially those birthed in Heaven and born in a dad or mom's heart.

"A new command I give you: Love one another. As I have loved you, so you must love one another. By this, everyone will know that you are my disciples if you love one another."
John 13:34-35, NIV

Question

How can you "mom" (or dad) on someone today?

Circle one:

A willingness

Open arms

A soft heart

God's love

Fearlessness

Or write your own

....

CHAPTER 31

DELIGHT

I had a convo with God. "Lord, I want to delight in you!" It sounded so grand. Delight meant SUNSHINE! I pictured roses, butterflies, rainbows and, of course, unicorns. Ahhh, it's so sweet to delight in the Lord.

I was coming into a busy season at work. I was fully deployed that month on an assignment at our headquarters. Delighting in God would be AWESOME! Especially since my schedule was brutal. In addition to that, I held the early shift, which meant I had to get up at 4. a.m. Could I do this? Yes! The Lord would send the butterflies to the airport to meet me!

I had my game face of delight ON. God was going to refresh me. He was going to make everyone play nice, act right, and there would surely be little blessings of delight everywhere I turned.

But then, it wasn't like that, and I wasn't delighted. Anybody else out there had a bad day? A bad season? Feel like life is working against you?

In the middle of my crazy month, my husband, who normally takes me to and from the airport, had to go out of town. That same night, my dog, Luke, had a TERRIBLE night with tummy problems. He was in such pain, and I was so so sad for him. I was crying, and he was frantic. It's not really cool to call in sick for your dog. They frown upon that. No canine sick time.

I was working on maybe one hour of sleep when my alarm went off to get up. "I don't know if I can do this, God. I need your help. Please refresh me and get me through this day. Please heal Luke and send your angels to comfort him."

I felt anything but delighted. I felt alone. Forgotten.

I got through the day. I wouldn't say it was with delight, but I felt His grace to get through it anyway. He sustained me as I kept drawing from Him with my little prayers.

That day, a woman came up to talk to my co-worker. She spoke about her dad dying two years ago and her mom passing away recently. She mentioned God and how important prayer was in her life. She had been taking care of her mom for the last year of her mom's life. She was peaceful with a smile on her face when she explained how good God had been to her. I'm normally the one who brings up Jesus on my Holy Spirit adventures, but here was this woman encouraging me. God HAD sent a butterfly to the airport. I knew it. I said, "Can I ask you a question? How do you delight in the Lord when someone you love is suffering?"

She shared that she also had a disabled adult daughter who lived with her. This woman KNEW secrets about delighting in the Lord. This butterfly's response to my question, "You are thankful for what you have. I thank God that my daughter has arms. That she can still hug me with those arms even though she can't walk. I thank God that I had that time with my mom at the end. When I think about her being gone, I immediately go to all the sweet times we had together. I don't think about the fact that I don't have her anymore. I thank God that I DID have her for the time that I did. Those are moments that I will forever hold in my memories." This woman had learned the art of delighting in the Lord and not focusing on what she didn't have. Jesus means we have sunshine hidden in our heart on a cloudy day. We aren't drawing from circumstances and always expecting to experience smooth sailing. We are internally steady on the rockiest cliff and the wildest seas. This butterfly had been through the darkness and emerged beautiful and untethered to the pain of it all.

I told the woman about my sweet puppy, and she exclaimed, "You need to learn puppy massage so you can comfort Luke when he is unwell."

I was like, "Puppy massage? There's a school for that?"

She laughed and said, "No, silly. You can look it up on YouTube!"

I know. I know. I was working on one hour of sleep, guys!

My husband was able to come home early from his trip because an appointment was canceled. Luke had a LITTLE bit better of a night. He was still uncomfortable. I practiced my fresh YouTube puppy massage skills, and he loved it!

But then I woke up the next morning with a full-blown migraine. I was still weary from lack of sleep, but I thought of what the woman said. I remembered to thank God for the goodness in my life. Instead of feeling punished, forgotten, unloved, and cursed, I said thank you. I thanked God that I had a head to hurt and that I was here and I had my family. Luke had a better night. These are all gifts to me. I redirected my thoughts to a grateful place rather than focusing on my pain and what I didn't have. I asked God to help me delight in Him that day and to refresh me. I realized I had been playing the 'what didn't go right game' for many years. It was a place of immaturity and ungratefulness, but man, God is just so so sweet to show me there was a place of peace and delight to rest in.

So I went to work with my headache. I considered staying home and resting, but I really felt like I was supposed to allow God to help me through the day at work. Sometimes, His message is REST for the body, and sometimes He is saying, "REST IN ME."

That day, a woman was talking to my co-worker. Once again, this lady brought up Jesus and prayer. He had sent me another butterfly! I asked her the same question, "What does it mean for you to delight in the Lord?"

She thought for a moment, "Trust. It means knowing that somehow He can and will work every situation out for good. We don't need to worry about it. He's got it covered!"

True. We can trust Him. We know that He has a big picture perspective that we may not have, but we can ask for His view. We can ask Him to help us see our situation in light of eternity.

Adventures in the Holy Spirit are not always full of sunshine and roses. He's teaching us and growing us up in the Spirit. It was time for me to grow up in gratitude. People are fickle. Things don't always go as planned. That friend, the husband, or job may let you down. Your money may disappear. Your body may not do what you want it to do. In this world, we will have trouble, but hope in God does not disappoint, my friend. So take heart; God has overcome this world. There's a place of delight in Him, come what may. I don't reside there, but I know how to find my way to it now. Someday, it will be my forever home.

"Make God the utmost delight and pleasure of your life, and He will provide for you what you desire the most. Give God the right to direct your life, and as you trust Him along the way you'll find He pulled it off perfectly! Quiet your heart in His presence and pray; keep hope alive as you long for God to come through for you..."
Psalm 37:4-7, TPT

Question

What do you need to delight yourself in the Lord?

Circle one:

Peace

Hope

Faith

To watch a YouTube video :)

A God hug

Or write your own

....

CHAPTER 32

PRAYING GRANDMAS

I stopped at a restaurant to have lunch. Two high-school-age girls sat chatting, and the table next to them was the only one available. I sat down and put my earbuds in because we were so close. I heard in my spirit about one of the girls, "She's so sweet and gentle, generous and kind, with a loving heart. She is going to be a great mom!"

I finished my lunch. I wanted to leave, but I felt like maybe I should share this encouraging word from the Holy Spirit. It was pretty simple, straightforward stuff that I assume most moms regularly share with their daughters. I pulled my earbuds out, and they were talking. As I said, we were in close proximity, and sometimes God gives me "spy ears" to hone in while in busy places. They were dropping F-bombs and cussing. This is probably the usual type of talk from teenagers, but I told God in my head, "I'm not sure sweet would be the word I would use to describe her." More like SASSY and SPUNKY! So, then, I began questioning everything I'd heard... I didn't want to say anything to her.

So I sat there, and I listened to her and her friend talking and cussing like sailors. Was I to pray it or say it?

I prayed for her, and I processed through the "what ifs." What if I don't deliver the word?

What if she was sad in her heart? She might need encouragement., or maybe the sweetness was hidden under the tough girl armor she wore.

As little girls growing up in a sometimes harsh world, we forget who we really are or hide it behind tough words and exteriors. These words spoken might have the power to call her higher and into her true destiny. They could remind her of who she really was created to be in her heart of hearts

What if she was going to have an unplanned pregnancy? This word might be her message from God that SHE COULD DO IT and would, in fact, be a GREAT MOM. A life would be "un-lived" if I took the easy way out. You already know that because of my two abortions, many times God sends me to women who are considering it. He plants the seed. Not one little one falls to the ground without Him knowing it.

High school girls can be intimidating. What if she was mean? She might cuss ME out? "What the bleep do you know, lady? Mind your business."

With all the "what ifs," I simply had to obey God. I still didn't know if I should share. My hesitancy was likely coming from the conversation I heard, not fitting with the "sweet and kind" words I'd heard for her.

So, I said, "Please, God, give me the courage to deliver this word if it is part of your plan."

At that precise moment, her friend got up and announced loudly, "I'm going to the bathroom. I will be back in a minute."

That was my "go" sign from the Holy Spirit. It was now or never! So I quickly wrote what I felt I heard on a note because I had a feeling she might want to read it again someday. I gave the note to her, and I also delivered the word to her directly. She did NOT cuss me out. In fact, she was so precious! She said, "I can't wait to show this to my mom. Thank you so much for giving this to me. Really. I so appreciate it. My name is Hannah, by the way." We talked for a quick minute, and then I saw her friend coming back. That was my cue to leave.

I went to fill up my drink before leaving, and a thought came to my mind out of nowhere. I thought of a little red Baptist church pamphlet about salvation. My grandmother gave it to me as a child. I could see her scribble on the cover. She had written on the front of it. "Jennifer-stay sweet," along with a few other treasured words. I teared up because I know my grandmother is the reason I love Jesus like I do.

I passed the table and said, "Bye, sweet girl." She asked if she could give me a hug. I remarked in our hug, "You know my grandmother wrote that to me, and I still have it. She wrote, "Jennifer-stay sweet," so no matter what comes your way, stay sweet, Hannah." She started crying. "My grandmother passed away two weeks ago. This means so much." Then I was crying again. Good Lord! I was so amazed at what God could do with such simple words and a small act of obedience in the midst of uncertainty.

TAKE AWAY:

Don't be deterred by outer appearances or even behaviors. God sees past all that to the heart, and this little one may have had a purer heart than another that looked outwardly perfect.

We are surrounded by a great cloud of witnesses cheering us on and even praying for us up in heaven. I sat down to write this blog and GUESS WHAT SONG CYCLED ON – "I can only imagine" the lyrics are about when we die and go to heaven.

I love that Hannah responded positively to the word, but we may not get a "confirmation" when we deliver messages from the Holy Spirit but trust it is a seed planted. That's happened to me many times. I share what I sense, and the person acts confused, or their face is bland. We can't let that deter us. Yes, I've doubted whether I really hear from God because of the lack of response, and we do need to check ourselves and our heart motives, but I've been walking with the Holy Spirit and practicing for a while, and I've learned: Only obey and stay connected to God. It's God's job to water the seed and make it grow in their life. I remember the woman who planted a seed in my life by giving me a devotional. I was NOT nice to her and thought she felt sorry for me.

We have to be willing to ACT on the divine appointments God brings to us. Ask Him to lead and guide your day and be aware of the little whispers and nudges. What if I had stopped short and NOT shared the part about my grandma? I thought the Holy Spirit brought the red pamphlet to mind, and I didn't brush it off. God gave me an opportunity to share it, and I didn't understand why until after I'd said it. Let the Holy Spirit have your tongue, and no second-guessing! Stay in the moment.

DELIVERY

For you, it may not be delivering a "word" or message from the Holy Spirit. What you share and bring from Heaven to earth through the Holy Spirit's guidance will be unique to your history and your gifts and heart. God gave us each a gift to share with the world! Maybe God has given you the gift of healing to deliver to someone, and you can pray for people, or it could be teaching a class or the Holy Spirit highlighting someone to be kind to or ask if they need prayer. Whatever you carry, be ready to deliver it and follow God's lead!

"Brothers and sisters, I want you to know about the gifts of the Holy Spirit. There are different kinds of gifts. But they are all given to believers by the same Spirit. The Holy Spirit is given to each of us in a special way. That is for the good of all. To some people, the Spirit gives a message of wisdom. To others, the same Spirit gives a message of knowledge. To others, the same Spirit gives faith. To others, that one Spirit gives gifts of healing. To others, he gives the power to do miracles. To others, he gives the ability to prophesy. To others, he gives the ability to tell the spirits apart. To others, he gives the ability to speak in different kinds of languages they had not known before. And to still others, he gives the ability to explain what was said in those languages...All the gifts are produced by one and the same Spirit. He gives gifts to each person, just as he decides.
1 Corinthians 12:1,4, 7-11, NIRV

"Pursue love and strive for spiritual gifts, but especially that you may prophesy."
1 Corinthians 14:1, AMP

Question

What do you need to operate in the gifts God has given you through the Holy Spirit? We all have at least one, the Bible says!

Circle one:

Boldness

Time with God to hear from Him

Trust

Faith

Activation of God's gifts

Or write your own

....

CHAPTER 33
ANGEL PINS

A fellow flight attendant and I introduced ourselves to each other. I noticed she was wearing a "broach." It's not really fashion-forward to wear "broaches" these days, but if you are in the airline business, it's one of the few ways you can bling the polyester wool blend suit. My mentor had given me an angel pin (broach) a few Christmases before. Interestingly enough, I came across it in my jewelry box that morning, so, I decided to wear it. It turned out to be a connection point led by the Holy Spirit.

Leighton and I admired each other's angel pins we were both sporting on our uniforms.

"So, do you love Jesus?" I asked.

"Oh, umm, this pin is a reminder of my dad. This is actually the first time I've worn it." Leighton went on to explain that her father had lost his life to cancer, and the pin was symbolic of hope for a cure. Her sister had given it to her after his passing.

We worked that day together. Leighton was a real team player, and I told her that. She was all over it by asking me what she could do to help set up the galley and insisting she do all the trash pick-ups. "My dad taught me that, and I played on a softball team, so it just comes naturally." She was a joy to work.

That night, I tucked myself into bed and read my favorite scriptures I have written on notecards. I travel with them and read them each night before bed. As I read the familiar and comforting truths, my mind was immediately attacked with voices. "What you just read, you know that's not true. God isn't with you. You are all alone. You have no one. No one would care if you lived or died, so just end it."

I felt so hopeless. I was depressed like a thousand pillows were squishing down on me and all my air out of the sails of my faith. I started crying. Finally, I took a breath, and I shook my head. The stuff I was hearing...It was all lies. I know the truth. I have God. I have my husband, kids, family. WHERE IS THIS COMING FROM? I fought back. Instead of going with the thoughts and allowing them to overcome me, I started speaking God's love over my life, "God is with me. He loves me. I am never alone." I read the scriptures again. I fought the oppression that tried to come again. After a few minutes in prayer, the feeling finally lifted.

The next day on the plane, Leighton and I chatted. I asked her how she liked her job, and we got to talking about her dad. She wore the white angel pin for him, and it represented lung cancer. When had he passed? Was it sudden?

She shared from her heart. "My dad was my rock. He was at all my softball games and was even my coach from the time I was a little girl. I went to college, and he was still at each and every one of my games. He never missed, but then he got sick, and he died so quickly. My mom actually left the country to work, and I have a sister, but she's married now."

And then I knew. I just knew the attack on my mind from the night before was how Leighton felt every day of her life since her dad died. So many times, our thoughts/feelings are more discernments that we, with Jesus and God's truths, have the power to overcome instead of allowing them to steal our joy. I was hearing the lies the enemy was telling her. Leighton didn't have her own faith, but I knew how to hold up the shield of faith in Jesus and stop these arrows. I am by no means "all there," but I had faced the battle she was facing, and I carried God's truth in my pocket. I looked at this precious girl and knew how much she had suffered at the hands of the enemy. My heart melted with empathy. She was injured and hurting. I could be a team player to her and pick her up when she was down.

I asked her gently, "Do you know if your dad loved Jesus?"

"I'm not sure," she said.

I wasn't 100% sure, but I had this impression that her dad was in heaven. Maybe he'd accepted Christ with his last breath. Maybe a nurse had prayed with him, for him. I didn't know, but I felt her dad was in heaven and wanted her to know about Jesus. His prayers for his daughter were the reason I was there. The authority and open door to speak into her life. The angel pins. A divine connection point. It was all orchestrated by her earthly and heavenly Father to reach Leighton's heart.

"Have you asked God where your dad is? No, I've never talked to God. I do want to know if there is a God since my dad is gone. I've been curious about religion since he died. I even took a class in college to try and figure it out. I was drawn to Buddhism because of the peace."

"I know this is kind of bold, and you can totally say no, but do you mind if we pray? If God is real, then He is perfectly capable of revealing Himself to you. He can show you who He is."

I shared a story with her about how, at one point, I was struggling if Jesus was the only way, and He answered me in no uncertain terms through a sermon, and showing me a scripture when I wasn't even trying to find one like that and then literally He took out a billboard sign! It said, "Jesus is the way!" and nothing else.

"So," I told Leighton, "I'm convinced, but I know he will reveal himself personally to you if we ask. And it won't be some religious lady on a plane telling you about him. You will know him yourself." "Yeah, I'd like to pray." So we sat heads bowed, holding hands on the jumpseat in the back of a Super 80 headed to Richmond, Va. I prayed she would have peace in her heart about her dad and God would be real to her.

I felt God's love for her, and there was definitely some mascara and snot wiping. We opened our eyes to find a lady standing in line waiting for the bathroom. A little embarrassing...but this older lady was so sweet. She said in a southern drawl, "Were you girls prayin'?" I said, "Yes, we were. We were praying that God would be real to Leighton."

She smiled and said, "Well, can I get in on this prayer?" Leighton and I laughed through tears, and we all grasped hands. This woman prayed for Leighton. It was such a sweet divine God moment. I felt so honored to be a momma in the faith.

A couple of months after we met, I felt led to send Leighton a Jesus Calling devotional. I see updates on Leighton, thanks to social media. She has a family now. She's married and has a precious baby. I don't know where she's at in her faith, but I'm not worried about it. I did my part. I planted the seed and sealed it with the blood of Jesus. It cannot be stolen. It will produce fruit in her life, by God.

"God did this so that they would seek him and perhaps reach out for him and find him, though he is not far from any one of us."
Acts 17:27, NIV

Question

How can you show hurting hearts the love of Christ?

Circle one:

Fearlessness

Hope

Kindness

Let go of a need to judge

Love

God's gift of discernment

Or write your own

....

CHAPTER 34

WEAR YOUR GOOD PJ'S

It was after midnight. I had tossed and turned in the hotel room bed for three hours, and I still couldn't sleep. The 4 a.m. pickup would come quickly.

I was finally asleep when I heard too-loud, laughing voices coming down the hallway. I looked at the red numbers on the hotel clock. It was 2 a.m. The voices got louder until they were right outside my door. Great. We were neighbors. They sounded drunk. I heard the play-by-play struggle as they were searching for the card key and trying to get it to work. Hush, please. I put a pillow over my head so it would go away. I did not need this right now.

Fact: Hotel walls are THIN. Even through my pillow, I could hear the tone of their voices change. Fun banter was turning into a hateful fight. He was yelling, accusing her of something. She was pleading, "No, I didn't do that. I promise!" They argued like that for several minutes. I prayed in my Holy Spirit prayer language, acknowledging that maybe God had put me in this room to intercede for them.

It escalated, and his voice was shouting. "Get the F out!" He repeated this over and over. She apologized and started crying, "I'm sorry. Please don't do this."

Finally, I heard the hotel room door slam. Good, they needed a time out, and maybe I could get some sleep, but then I heard her right outside my door sobbing. Wailing. She wasn't leaving.

I laid in the bed. The guy was angry, really angry. I reminded myself this was none of my business. Still, I asked God, "What do you want me to do? Call security?"

Jesus talks about being moved with compassion, and I just couldn't stay in bed and listen to her cry like that right outside my hotel room door.

I opened my door and peeked out. If I could describe this: She was on her knees in the fetal position with her forehead touching that nasty hotel hallway floor that had probably never been cleaned. She reminded me of the woman who cried tears on Jesus's feet and dried them with her own hair.

I leaned down and put my hand on her shoulder as she cried, and I prayed underneath my breath. I then said something along these lines, "I'm so so sorry you were talked to that way...You are worthy of love and to be spoken to kindly." I petted her hair and told her that she wasn't alone. God was with her, and this could be her line in the sand moment to take his hand, and everything could change for her.

She never looked up, but her cry was softer now.

A baby-faced twenty-ish-year-old security guard barreled out of the elevators, "What happened? Is she hurt?"

He had it from there, so I patted her one last time, "Just stick with Jesus and never let go."

I got off my knees realizing I had locked myself out of my room! This, my friends, is why you always wear your good pajamas because you just never know.

The security guard let me back in, and then I heard him through the door, requesting they be respectful of the other guests and asking if there would be any further problems.

Their voices were quieter, but they still argued, and he continued to tell her to get the F out. She said, "Please stop yelling." When she responded now, she had a strength in her voice that I hadn't heard before. I knew it was Jesus.

I prayed again in the Holy Spirit. I also prayed she would turn to Jesus and never let go. I heard the door close again, and it sounded like she left. I continued to pray for both of them until I fell asleep, and the next thing I knew, my alarm was going off. Yay, now I get to work a three-leg, twelve-hour day!

What I took away from this Holy Spirit adventure:

We are all messengers of hope. You carry Jesus, and He is a living hope. He lives in you and flows through you like a river to the world around you, changing atmospheres, establishing peace, being arms of comfort, releasing His joy, love, and resources.

1.   **Messengers have divinely created appointments.**
        God placed me in THAT room, and it was a divine appointment. I was
        inconvenienced. I was TIRED, but I have told God I would be obedient
        after missing some other opportunities. I wasn't happy about it, but I was
        willing. I did what He asked of me. You don't have to be a flight attendant
        or travel. Divine appointments are along the path that God sets for
        us. We can ask, morning by morning, to be sent to those who need a
        message from Him.

2.   **Messengers are seed planters.**
        We plant the seed, but God makes it grow. I never even saw this
        woman's face, but I pray that my touch carried His love, and one day in
        Heaven, I will see her again. I didn't see any immediate breakthrough, but
        I'm not responsible for that part of the process. God is.

3.   **Messengers have God's love.**
        God can't trust messengers who don't have love in their hearts for all.
        The more I acknowledge my own sin and am healed and loved by God,
        the less others' sins seem so insurmountable. I mean, I didn't really like the
        way the guy was talking, but I didn't condemn him either. Pre-Jesus, my life
        was a train wreck. I've been in relationships like this where you are saying
        and doing things out of a wounded heart. How much must he hate himself
        to reject her this way? I was SO thankful he didn't open that door, and I
        don't really know what I would say or do if he had, but it might be along
        the lines of, "What you said really hurt her heart, and I know that's not who
        you really are or the man you want to be, is it?" The kingdom of darkness
        bows to God's love and light.

*"After this, the Lord appointed seventy-two others and SENT them. "The harvest is
plentiful, but the workers are few. Go! I am sending you out like lambs among wolves…
He replied, "I saw Satan fall like lightning from heaven. I have given you authority to
trample on snakes and scorpions and to overcome all the power of the enemy; nothing
will harm you."*
Luke 10: 8, 18-19, NIV

*"But we have this treasure in jars of clay to show that this all-surpassing power is from God
and not from us."*
2 Corinthians 4:7, NIV

Question

What do you need to see past the sin and into the original design of others?

Circle one:

Mercy

Compassion

Fearlessness

Removal of judgment for your own sins

A purified heart

Or write your own

....

CHAPTER 35

IRELAND

My husband and I received round-trip positive space tickets from the airlines. I asked the Holy Spirit for direction. We were throwing out a lot of destinations that made sense for us:

England—My husband's mom was born there and came to America when she married.

Finland—We could see the northern lights from a glass igloo.

Australia: They shut down our local Outback Restaurant. Where else could I get authentic Australian food? It made sense to take a fourteen-hour trip across the world.

I prayed that morning and kept my eyes peeled for any nudges.

The first sign: I was trying to make reservations for a restaurant in Fort Worth. It brought up Cork, Ireland, as a city to search. Ireland? That was odd...or maybe it was God. I asked for continued confirmation.

It seemed like the Holy Spirit began highlighting things about Ireland, not to mention that I recently found out I am 53.9% British and Irish. Jesus cares about genealogy. It's mentioned throughout the Bible, old and new testament.

There were many confirmations for Ireland, and my husband was on board. It was fun to know that this was God's plan and not mine.

So Ireland it was!

We did a whirlwind driving tour of Ireland. One day near Killarney, Ireland, we decided we were going to visit Ross Castle. We got up that morning with this destination in mind as we drove on the crazy, narrow Irish roadways in a stick shift on the wrong side of the road with the steering wheel on the wrong side of the car! Whew! My help at navigating was critical. I plugged "Ross Castle" into the GPS, and off we went.

"You have arrived," said the female navigation robot voice with an Irish lilt.

We were confused when we saw the fenced and very old hospital. "It says to turn into this hospital, but that can't be right?"

"Maybe Ross Castle is on the other side?" I said at my navigation fail. I looked around. But this was a hospital. Maybe they moved the castle? Or maybe this was the original site or something.

OR maybe we are supposed to be here. I asked my husband what he thought. It might be a prayer opportunity. He and I don't operate the same way with the Holy Spirit, but he was game to pray.

I read the sign, "St. Finian's Hospital." The facility was surrounded by razor wire, but the gates were open, so we could drive in. It felt like an open door from God. I googled it. An online article said it was formerly a boys' mental health facility called a "lunatic asylum." I looked up Saint Finian, the hospital's namesake. He was an early Irish saint credited with founding a church and monastery. He cured a young boy of leprosy and separated himself in purity to God.

Yeah, I felt it in my Spirit. I was supposed to be here.

My husband and I prayed as we drove a circle around the hospital's grounds. At first, I was a little creeped out. I realized as I read the news articles online about the poor facilities, treatment, and abuse of the young men being the reason behind the shutdown and now abandoned facility. This place was a house of horrors. Still, I felt the intentionality of God leading us. I turned up my worship music, and the lyrics sang out "Abba," which means Father. As I prayed, I felt the peace of God and his ability to transform even the worst situation from ashes to beauty. God was spiritually cleaning the house in preparation for something brand new here.

When we drove out, I looked at the GPS. It said we were now ten minutes from Ross Castle. WHAT? For me, there is no other explanation than the divine leading of God.

I was so excited, yet not really surprised, when we arrived at the real Ross Castle. While there, we heard about a boat ride we could take to a small twenty-one-acre island. It was called "Innisfallen Island. In 640 AD, none other than St Finian chose to live and separate himself to God and teach other young men there. We basically had the island to ourselves without interruption. Words can't describe the awesome beauty and peace I felt from God. I cried because I felt

God's heart there, and I considered it a great honor to be where men separated themselves to be closer to God.

When I returned home, I was reading the Bible, and I asked God, "I had a blast, but did anything really get accomplished in Ireland?" I didn't convert anyone. I didn't share any prophetic words. I had a great time seeing God's beautiful creation and enjoying quality time with my husband. I don't always hear Him clearly. I feel more nudges, but, that morning, I heard so clearly, "Prayers heal the land."

There was nothing on my GPS that should have connected Ross Castle to a psychiatric hospital to Saint Finian, but God knew the connection. Finian was a man who had given his life as a devoted follower and, almost 1400 years later, his name still mattered to God. His feet walked the very place I walked and spread the good news of peace. The prayers he prayed still existed, and my husband and I were able to agree in prayer and say still, even now, "Yes and Amen," to what God was saying over that land.

If you want a Holy Spirit adventure, pray before you make plans and wait on His confirmations. Don't be on auto pilot. Let Jesus take the wheel and ask the Holy Spirit to lead you today. Logic, or the need for something to make sense, is one of the biggest roadblocks from experiencing a Holy Spirit adventure. If we rely on logic and then something doesn't make sense, we discount it or get stuck and refuse to keep going in faith.

Take his hand and hold on. He has so much to show you as you let Him lead!

"Every place on which the sole of your foot treads shall be yours..."
Deuteronomy 11:24, ESV

"So shall my word be that goes out from my mouth; it shall not return to me empty, but it shall accomplish that which I purpose, and shall succeed in the thing for which I sent it."
Isaiah 55:11, ESV

Question

How can you let go of logic and let God lead you today?

Circle one:

Prayer

Trust

Faith

Holy Spirit power

The mind of Christ

Submission to God

Or write your own

....

CHAPTER 36

GIVE GOD FIVE MINUTES

I was off to Austin for an ODAN (on duty all night). It is 'kind of' a sweet trip. I'm only gone about ten hours or so from home. I land about ten PM and then leave first thing in the morning.

The not-so-sweet: The time available for sleeping is usually less than five hours on these trips, and I need nine or ten hours to function with a smile.

I always know, with God, there's a Holy Spirit adventure to be had, though. He is strategic in our lives on timing and location, but there wouldn't be much time for an adventure this go-round with five or less hours of zzz's.

I got to my room, and the door wouldn't lock. I was too tired to worry about it. I pushed a chair up to the door.

Feeling the pressure of time, I did the usual drill quickly. I powered down and laid everything out for the next day on one of the queen-sized beds like I did when I was in elementary school as if it was a fully dressed person laying there. I got in my PJs. I pulled out my Fly Girl Journal that I use to chronicle my prayers over the cities God sends me to. I wrote a few things down in faith that came to mind.

To be honest, I wasn't really feeling it. Sometimes, I feel super anointed and like the Spirit is flowing. During those moments, I feel like I'm flying in the Spirit above all the chaos and noise of my life, and I feel His peace. I know that I'm sent on an assignment, but sometimes I just don't feel a thing and wonder if He's even there.

I opened my Bible and read some scriptures that didn't seem to fit or resonate in my Spirit. I usually try to decree the word of God over the cities I visit. There would be no time to do that in the morning. I pulled the chains for the blinds, but they didn't budge. Oh well. I would be up before sunrise anyway. I wanted to feel God and sense His leading me, but I didn't. I just felt annoyed and tired.

I walked into my bathroom and there was a six-foot puddle of water surrounding the toilet. How could I not have noticed that before?

GREEEEAAAAAAT. Just great.

I called down to the front desk and said I needed a new room. They weren't sure if they had one. They would check and call me back. I started packing up because I wasn't staying here. I sat on my bed feeling pretty bummed about things not going as planned.

I finally got to my new room. The door lock worked. There was no potty water on the floor. I checked the blinds. They closed without issue. Well, at least there was that.

I unpacked AGAIN.

I set my alarm for 5 a.m. That only left me five minutes with God in the morning. It was all I had but sleep didn't come quickly and that made me anxious because I knew I had to get up early.

It felt too early when my alarm sang out. I didn't know how I wanted to spend my five minutes with God. I normally read a page out of the Bible.

I closed my eyes. I still wasn't feeling this was a God-led adventure at all and probably just a dumb trip that would steal the rest of my day due to a lack of sleep.

I huffed and decided to turn worship music on and rest with God, but when the song came on, I felt God's presence fill the room. The lyrics sang out, "Spirit lead me." The words were stirring my heart, and then I couldn't stay sleepy. I felt God take my hand, and I was moved to dance.

"This is my worship
This is my offering
In every moment
I withhold nothing
I'm learning to trust You
Even when I can't see it
And even in suffering
I have to believe it
If You say "it's wrong," then I'll say "no"
If You say "release," I'm letting go
If You're in it with me, I'll begin

And when You say to jump, I'm diving in
If You say "be still ," then I will wait
If You say to trust, I will obey
I don't wanna follow my own ways
I'm done chasing feelings
Spirit lead me."
By Influence Music

I opened the blinds, and I sang.

The lyrics were from Heaven and Him, and they filled the room and created something beautiful to be sent out over the city.

As I danced and worshiped my creator, I felt the power of God flowing through me like a mighty rushing river.

I opened my Bible and went to the window and read the words on the page out over the city:

"But as soon as they were at rest, they again did what was evil in your sight. Then, you abandoned them to the hand of their enemies so that they ruled over them. And when they cried out to you again, you heard from heaven, and in your compassion, you delivered them time after time."
Nehemiah 9:28, NIV

On and on, Nehemiah goes in this chapter about us losing our way and then crying out for God to hear and us and respond to our cries and then rescuing us. These were different people but the same problems we all encounter today by wanting to go back to the familiar. I stood in front of the window and prayed over Austin for God to forgive us and be compassionate once again. I spoke the lyrics from the song, "Spirit lead me. Spirit lead Austin."

My timer went off. It seemed like I had been in worship for quite some time, but it had only been five minutes. I looked at my phone, and a friend had sent me a podcast to watch. I pressed play while I did my makeup. The woman said she'd learned to stop trying to make her own plans and, instead, to simply follow God's voice and be obedient to Him. She said she'd learned to listen for and "let the spirit lead me." I stopped mid-mascara stroke. "Spirit lead me" The same lyrics in the song. Only God.

WHAT I LEARNED

1. **Things don't always go as planned, but it doesn't mean God isn't with you.**

   What if the room I was assigned wasn't in the right location to decree things over the city? Sometimes, we don't understand what God is doing. Why are there so many roadblocks? We have to trust that God is positioning us for victory and favor and rerouting us around the roadblocks. Sometimes, He needs our own personal strength to be exhausted so He can be large and in charge. Then it's not our power or passion but His own. When we are weak, that allows Him to be strong in us. He empties us. Not to punish us, but so he can fill us with himself.

2. **Worship is warfare, and it awakens our sleepy spirits and spiritually sleepy cities.**

   He's with us even when we cannot feel His presence. There is so much going on in the spiritual realm we cannot perceive! The lyrics in the song said, "I'm done chasing feelings." I was feeling God after my spirit was awakened. What if I had listened to my sleepy, achy body that morning? What if I'd allowed my disappointment to sever my connection because my time the night before didn't 'feel' anointed? I had a need for perseverance.

3. **Give God five minutes a day.**

   Even when you're tired. Even when you don't think you have it to give. Let the Holy Spirit lead and go on a God adventure!

"Patient endurance is what you need now so that you will continue to do God's will. Then you will receive all that he has promised."
Hebrews 10:36, NLT

"The winds are your messengers; flames of fire are your servants."
Psalm 104:4, NLT

Question

What do you need to go on a Holy Spirit adventure even when you aren't feeling it?

Circle one:

Faith

Perseverance

Strength

Grace

God's help

Or write your own

....

CHAPTER 37

WHEN GOD TAKES A CITY

It was my first day on call for reserve. I was expecting a slow month, so I was surprised at the notification of my assignment as my cellphone made the familiar ding.

Bleh, a three-day. I looked at the trip. It had a twenty-nine hour layover in Columbus, OH. Not the most exciting place to go to, but the trip wasn't bad. I reminded myself I had written out a prayer for my reserve month before it began: God send me where you want me to go. If I get a trip, I will know that it is from you for divine purpose.

I woke up the next morning to spend the whole day in downtown Columbus. I wanted to find some good grub and prayer walk, which is my usual Holy Spirit adventure plan.

I headed out, plugged in my earbuds with worship, and asked the Holy Spirit to lead me. I kept passing so many beautiful people. They were homeless. I stopped in my tracks at the worthiness of their hearts. Seriously, it was as if the Holy Spirit had given me new glasses, and I could see them, really see them. God had been breaking my heart in the previous season with dead dogs, betrayals by friends, and feeling unloved. My heart was softer and pliable. I have NEVER gone around asking people if I could take pictures, but then again, I've never been so captivated and drawn to do so. When I asked before I took a picture, each person smiled. Not one person asked me for money. One man wanted to put his cigarette down, but I said, "God loves you as you are," so he kept it. He sees past our shame and loves us the same.

I saw a church on the corner with a sign out front that said all were welcome. I saw a man hunched over as I opened the gate. His head was bent so awkwardly. "Downcast" was the word that came to mind. There was another homeless person in the gated entry, and she was dressed in a short skirt and sequins. She smiled at me, and I thought she might be an angel.

I internally asked the Holy Spirit if I had permission to go into this church, and I felt a 'yes' in my Spirit. I put the full armor of God on.

I walked into the church, and I saw dozens of bodies lying covered up on the pews. This was a safe haven for the homeless to come in from the cold and sleep in peace. Tears leaked down my face. A man sat on the third row. I stopped. What if he was dangerous? I was losing my Jesus glasses, and fear was gripping my new heart, turning it cold. He immediately got up and turned towards me. I was standing in the middle of the aisle.

I froze. I could turn and run, and I wanted to, as he headed straight towards me in a very determined manner. I felt defenseless. I flinched and braced myself. He growled and grunted as he walked past me. It was all I could do not to turn around and see if he was coming back to harm me. He walked back past me, not stopping, and took a seat again in the third row with his back to me. I stood there shaking. I reminded myself I had God's permission to be here. I got my Jesus glasses back. I felt His peace wash over me. I was safe. Worship lyrics played through my headphones in my ear, "Find me here in everything that's hopeless in every part that's broken when my heart is cut wide open...among the chaos, You speak. I'm overwhelmed by your peace..."

I felt the holy awe of God. He was right here in the midst of the broken. I stopped and knelt, and then I got down on my face, nose to the ground in the church, and I worshipped God and asked him to help. I asked him to fill this place with Himself.

I got up off the floor and looked at the back of the growling man's head, and prayed for him.

I heard, "Go ask him if he needs prayer."

I argued back, "What? Remember, God, he growled at me. He means me harm." The familiar fear was there again.

I heard it again, "Go ask him if he needs prayer."

I began shaking again, and I'm ashamed to say I held on to my backpack tighter. I slowly walked towards him and then stopped. I saw him looking at a phone with a picture of a little girl on the screen saver, and my heart softened. My voice breaking I softly said to the man, "Do you need prayer for anything?"

He said in a kind voice, "Let me think... I actually just woke up." Such a normal response. "Could I pray for a blessing over you and your life?"

"Sure. That would be great. Thank you."

I asked him if I could put my hand on his shoulder, and he nodded. I touched his hoodie, "Jesus, this is your son, and you love him. Give him a fresh start and bless him in every way. Bring him back to his family and cover him with your grace."

I sensed the reason I was here had been satisfied, so I walked out into the sun as tears streamed down my face. I had been so afraid. I know this is white-girl-sheltered problems, but I am being honest about my immaturity in love. God would bless it, not because of my perfect performance, but because I obeyed.

I met another woman that day a few steps away from the church on the steps of the Ohio Statehouse. Dymonica is a mentor and tutor for at-risk youth for an organization called "City Life." God said she would be a mother to nations, and we agreed in prayer over the city and the youth.

When God takes a city, does he go to the leaders? Yes, but you might be surprised whom He considers a leader. When God takes a city, does he send an army? Yes, his angels are surrounding us to bring His Kingdom of Heaven, and He just needs a willing heart. You are sent to every location you go to on a divine assignment. He is sending you. Will you say yes?

"God dwells in that city; it cannot be destroyed. From the very break of day, God will protect it."
Psalm 46:5, NLT

"Brothers and sisters, consider who you were when God called you to salvation. Not many of you were wise scholars by human standards, nor were many of you in positions of power. Not many of you were considered the elite when you answered God's call. But God chose those whom the world considers foolish to shame those who think they are wise, and God chose the puny and powerless to shame the high and mighty. He chose the lowly, the laughable in the world's eyes—nobodies—so that he would shame the somebodies. For he chose what is regarded as insignificant in order to supersede what is regarded as prominent."
1 Corinthians 1:26-28, TPT

"The LORD is close to the brokenhearted and saves those who are crushed in spirit."
Psalm 34:18, NIV

"So he returned home to his Father. And while he was still a long way off, his Father saw him coming. Filled with love and compassion, He ran to his son, embraced him, and kissed him."
Luke 15:20, NLT

"This is the confidence we have in approaching God: that if we ask anything according to his will, he hears us."
1 John 5:14, NIV

Question

What do you need to see the world differently as God wants you
to see it?

Circle one:

Help

Courage

A soft heart

Eyes for God's beauty

Love

Or write your own

....

CHAPTER 38

HOLY SPIRIT
ADVENTURES IN PRAYER

It was the last day of a three-day trip, and I knew I had a special package to deliver, but I didn't know who it was for. As I was preparing for my trip, my eyes were drawn to the gift. It was a devotional called "Adventures in Prayer" by Pastor Mary Jo Pierce.

Mary Jo is a very wise woman and prayer pastor. She put a forty-day devotional book together. I inquired about getting a few of them to give away as the Holy Spirit led. Mary Jo was once a flight attendant and shares about that in her prayer journey written in the book. When I asked, she kindly agreed to sign them and wrote a different prophetic word in each of them. Mary Jo has planted seeds in me and so many others with her teachings and wisdom.

I came across one of the devotionals the night before my trip. The Holy Spirit nudged me and said, "Take it." So I put it in my suitcase, having the impression that someone along my trip might need the encouragement.

I met the crew and fell in love with one of the flight attendants in the back. We will call her Lilly. She was beautiful and very loving and kind. We talked about God and life. Her faith really encouraged me.

Towards the end of my trip, I was reminded about the devotional in my suitcase. I said, "God, the book is for Lilly, right?"

Lilly was standing right in front of me along with another flight attendant. Her name was Ella. Ella was quiet but a little micromanaging on how I handled the galley. She was probably in her early 60's. She was not unkind or rude, but I sensed a void and lack of joy though she'd said very little. I heard in my spirit, "Give it to Ella."

So I waited until Ella and I were alone in the front galley. "I have something for you." I pulled out the journal. I shared the author's story and how I came about having it. "I felt like God said this was for you if you would like to have it."

Ella was a little intimidating, and I wouldn't have been surprised if she declined the gift. I continued on a little flustered when her face stayed impassive. I said, "Ummm, the author signed it and wrote something." I opened it up and read the message written so many months earlier.

Ella's blank stare changed to shock as she took the book from my hands and read the message. She started crying. "Yes, this is for me from God."

Ella hadn't spoken about anything personal up to that point. She took the journal and began sharing about her life as we sat on the jumpseat together.

Ella shared that she'd gone through a very messy divorce, but she met a man on the plane a year before. They were taking it very slowly. He would retire soon, and they had spoken about a future life together. She also shared she was going on an "adventure" of her own to New Zealand and Australia. She would be leaving in five days and would be on her own a lot of the trip. She was meeting up with some family along the way. It was the first time she'd done anything like it. Ella was nervous going alone and driving around in unfamiliar places, but this book so appropriately called "Adventures in Prayer" would be with her on her own big adventure (her words).

"God is with you!" I exclaimed, "You are not really alone." She hugged me and said, "Thank you."

We were almost home, but I saw an immediate change in Ella. Her whole countenance changed. The frown she had most of the trip was turned upside down. She was beaming.

We are just God's messengers doing what He says, and if we listen and obey, we can get the message to the right person at the right place and on time. Our willingness to hear and follow the little whispers can change someone's day and perhaps their life.

QUESTIONS

What if I had let Ella's bristly demeanor offend me and built a wall in my heart to keep her out? I would not have been inclined to give a gift to someone I didn't like. If I only wanted to share hope with someone like me, I would have given it to Lilly. While lovely, Lilly was not who God had in mind. He leaves the ninety-nine for the lost single one.

Do you find yourself responding to people by the way they act rather than by what God is saying to you about them? Do you allow it to intimidate you? Or maybe you are super bold and blowing past some of God's stop signs to pray first and allow Him to lead you and guide you?

Remember, we are carriers and messengers of hope. Are you scheduled to make a delivery of God's kind of hope to someone today with your smile, with a kind word, gift, or a helping hand?

"We now have this light shining in our hearts, but we ourselves are like fragile clay jars containing this great treasure. This makes it clear that our great power is from God, not from ourselves."
2 Corinthians 4:7, NLT

Question

What do I need from God to be in step with the Holy Spirit and have adventures with Him?

Circle one:

Faith over fear

Wisdom

Trust

To sit in His presence

Or write your own

....

CHAPTER 39

WHEN IT COSTS US

My daughter and I were flying back from Paris as non-revs. It's a perk of working in the airline biz. The problem with non-reving is you always fly standby. Flights are overbooked in the summer. It can be very stressful. We made it to Paris without an issue but coming back was a different story.

My daughter and I showed up early for our flight home, but another flight had been canceled, which left our flight with more than fifty people on the standby list.

We quickly listed on a different flight to Boston. It wasn't looking great either. While in line, I overheard a mother and daughter's stressed conversation. They were bickering and snipping at each other about various things. They were also non-revving and had already been stuck in Paris for three days trying to get out.

After waiting patiently behind everyone who purchased real tickets, we finally heard the gate agent call our names. It was music to our ears. We were handed our tickets and could finally board the plane.

We were so grateful to see our seats were assigned in Business Class. This meant lay-down beds, amenity kits, personal entertainment systems, and all the fun pampering and gourmet food. YEAH GOD!

I was 'jetting' for the plane when I saw the mother and daughter from earlier. They were having a conversation with the gate agent and looked really upset.

The mom said, "What do you mean you only have one ticket? My daughter is only fifteen years old, so I can't leave her or let her go without me. Please, please, I'm begging you. I will pay. I don't care what it costs."

The daughter pleaded with the gate agent, "Isn't there something you can do?"

The gate agent said in her French accent, "I'm sorry, Mademoiselle, but there is nothing. Would you like to take the one ticket? It is the last seat."

I could have walked on and pretended I didn't hear their conversation. It wasn't my problem.

As a flight attendant, I could give my seat to her and offer to take the 7+ hour flight sitting on an uncomfortable jumpseat. The jumpseat had no nice fluffy cushion, no recline button, there would be no hot towels, no warm nuts, and NO Bose knock-off headphones! There would be no sleep for me on a jumpseat.

I felt a Holy Spirit conviction. My heart sunk when I thought of giving up my penthouse for a tiny doghouse. I would be going from Business Class to a 12" by 12" metal square with minimal cushion and zero personal space. Still, I was in a position to help. I prayed. I could say it was an easy decision, but it was not.

The Holy Spirit wasn't telling me what to do in this situation. He was not manipulating me but ASKING if I was willing to give up my place for these two to have any place at all. I felt that God would be pleased if I did it. I love to make my Father in Heaven smile and laugh. There would be no punishment or guilt trip if I said no. He wouldn't be disappointed in me. It was MY choice.

I turned around midway down the jet bridge and went back to the gate. With mixed emotions, I motioned to the gate agent. I handed her my business class ticket. I said, "I can take the jumpseat if it helps them both make the flight." The mother looked at me, confused. She wanted to know why I would do this. Could she pay me?

I answered, "God did this for you. He loves you and is going to take care of you. Please just tell God thank you because you need to know He is the reason why I did it."

The mom and daughter both began crying and hugging me.

It's so much fun being a part of what God is doing in others' lives, but sometimes, it can cost us a price personally.

Would this mom have done the switch-a-roo for me if she was presented with the same choice? No, she confessed when she came to the back of the plane from her nice cozy seat. She wanted to say thanks again, but I didn't do it for her.

"I did it because God gave me an opportunity to help," I explained. I knew that decision would eventually bring me joy.

The jumpseat wasn't the worst thing in the world, of course, but it was extremely uncomfortable. My daughter and I had trouble getting home from Boston, but we DID make it back.

I wouldn't change a thing. I'm glad I made the switch. My reward may not be here on this earth. The Holy Spirit may lead us to be generous with our heart, time or give something up so another won't be left behind, and it can cost us. These opportunities refine our hearts when we are willing to suffer and show love on our adventures with the Holy Spirit. We want to look like Him. We pick up His cross. Not out of compulsion but out of a heart that desires to be made in His image.

"Love the Lord your God with all your heart and with all your soul and with all your mind and with all your strength. The second is this: Love your neighbor as yourself. There is no commandment greater than these."
Mark 12:30-31, NIV

Question

What do I need from God to be willing to give from my heart freely?

Circle one:

God's grace

God's giving heart

God's generous spirit

Gratitude

Perspective

Or write your own

....

CHAPTER 40

ROLLIN' WITH
SEAL TEAM SIX

I received a notification that said, "RELEASED" for the next day. A few minutes later, my phone rang, "Flight Attendant Weiss, we gave you an assignment that is leaving tonight."

"What happened to my release for tomorrow?"

"Oh, yeah, we took that away."

I looked at the trip. The departure was close to midnight. It was a simple trip. It was a turn to Austin, but it meant that I would be by myself for the weekend.

I fought the discouragement of the bait and switch of a release and the desire to be home with my family. Then I had another idea. I was staying in one of my favorite hotels in Austin, and I had an eighteen-hour layover there. It WAS the weekend, so maybe my husband would want to go and explore with me.

I called my husband and asked him to join me, but he said, "I think I'll stay here and work around the house." I was disappointed.

I arrived at the plane for the late-night departure. We crossed paths with the flight attendants who flew the plane in as they were leaving the aircraft. They were not happy campers and said, "I do not know why you are here."

Thanks, glad to see you too, and by the way, I don't really want to BE HERE! Let's just call scheduling and sort this out. It was past my bedtime. My draw-string pants were waiting. I wanted to say this, but I kept silent.

The other flight attendant by her side said, "This is some bull-'bleep.' I'm calling our union. We were on this trip and, for NO reason, crew scheduling took us off and assigned you guys on reserve to go to Austin. So, instead of a cool hotel and having fun in Austin, we are staying at some dump in Dallas."

"Well, call scheduling," one of the other reserves said.

"We did. They refused to give us the trip back!" she said smartly.

My Holy spirit antenna went up. God pulled some major strings to get me to Austin. I felt the importance. This wasn't some trip I was handed without regard for my sleep or comfort. I had a purpose. I have to admit I felt a little like Seal Team Six being called in to take out Bin Laden, but I really wasn't sure what exactly the mission was.

It was an easy and short flight. Most passengers slept.

Later, at the hotel, bleary-eyed at 2 am, I wrote some prayers down I sensed from the Holy Spirit for Austin in my "Fly Girl Journal."

I woke up the next morning in my swanky hotel. God had really sent me in style this time. I planned my day; first, get some great food, then walk it off in prayer around the Capitol.

Normally, when in Austin, I just truck on inside the gates to the Capitol and begin worshipping and praying. This time I felt a strong caution from the Holy Spirit.

I stood in front of the gates of the Texas State Capitol. I felt the distinct impression that I would have to be in TUNE with the Holy Spirit. If I didn't listen, moment by moment, the mission would be aborted or fail. I stayed outside the gates in obedience. I walked around the outer perimeter of the Capitol. I listened to Rita Springer's "Battles" CD, and I sang it quietly to God. As I passed another entry gate, I looked up to God and asked, "Now?" I heard a gentle whisper on the wind say, "Not Yet."

The lyrics were speaking to my heart. The words rang as truth, "Every Battle is Yours... And all I did was Praise, and all I did was worship...Great Defender...so much better your way." I was walking and praying outside the gates, sending my love to God and being obedient. IT WAS POWERFUL. I could feel it. There was a gentle pressure of a hand on my shoulder that was guiding me. I felt so safe with that touch. I was tucked right under the shadow of His wing.

I came to another gate. I asked, "Enter now, Lord?"

Still, I heard, "Not yet." I didn't understand it, but I obeyed.

I looked up and realized I was back where I started. I had walked around the entire perimeter.

I hit shuffle, and a song came blasting through my headphones, singing, "Let's start a war! Let's start a love war!"

It was a major change in the tempo from the peaceful worship songs that cycled through on my long walk.

I heard the Holy Spirit as clear as day: "NOW!"

I was confused. "Okay, what exactly do I do now?"

(Do you remember the scene in Brave Heart when the opposing army is charging straight towards Brave Heart and his army on the battlefield? William Wallace chants, "HOLD.....HOLD! HOLD!" And then when Wallace calls out "NOW!" At Wallace's command, his army drops their position of defense by lowering their shields. As a surprise to their enemy, they unexpectedly pick up their weapons. The enemy had no time to react but ran right into their spears.)

I had been "holding." It had to be the right moment, and apparently, that moment was NOW.

I looked in front of me. A guy and girl were walking into the Capitol grounds. I chuckled. The back of his shirt said, "Get Your Guns Up." This saying is the Texas Tech University motto. I didn't have a gun, but I got my worship on. The weapons we wage war with are not the weapons of this world. We enter His gates with thanksgiving and praise.

It was seriously like I had to get in there right that second. I know this sounds a little 'drama,' but I felt like the moment where the seal team ropes in, except it was just me with my flips flops and sweaty armpits. God's angel armies were in the battle. Worship was the doorway for Heaven's army to enter. I followed that couple through the gates. SO MUCH HAPPENED inside those gates that I couldn't write it without it being a book. I will share some of it.

I went in and, at first, all was quiet. I was still listening to worship music. I jotted down some of the lyrics from different artists. I felt like the words in the lyrics were commanding the atmosphere around our State Capitol to change.

I sang out along with the lyrics quietly.

"We release the sound to break through the atmosphere, and we release it now.

Your people call you near...

Could this be the hour?

Could this be the day of new beginnings?

Could this be the time?

In our generation."

"There is a blood that cost a life to pay my way.

Death its price when it flowed down from the cross, my sins were gone.

My sins forgot."

These words flowed through my headphones from Rita Springer

After walking for almost a solid hour inside the gates, I found myself at the Capitol steps, and people were streaming inside.

I had another strong impression that I was not to enter. I heard in my head, "Not yet. We haven't taken the entrance yet."

I normally don't hear God with such clarity, so I thought I might be hearing things. Did I need to wait or keep moving? My eyes settled on one of those orange construction cones tucked in and out of the corner of the deep windows of the Capitol building. It really had no reason for being there. I felt like God was saying, "Caution."

I moved to some steps on the side of the building. I sat there waiting for God's angels to do whatever they were doing. Meanwhile, I wasn't SAYING anything to the enemy I was worshiping. Deep in prayer, asking for the things that came to mind for our beautiful state.

I heard a voice again, "Turn the worship music on."

I responded, "Check! Already done."

I heard, "No, out loud."

There were tours going on, and it was a Saturday. I was in Austin, and there were LOTS of people.

I sat on the steps and turned the music on really low.

I heard, "Louder!"

I have a thing about loud noises. My freedom can't infringe on others negatively.

I heard it again, though, "LOUDER!"

I looked around, and at that moment, there was NO ONE around me. A confirmation from God, and a little help through circumstance to be obedient.

I increased the volume. I am not kidding, a black crow flew from the side straight at me. I saw it in slow motion, and it truly scared me. I threw my hands up in front of me. Thankfully, there was a rail between the bird and me. It landed close to me but still on the other side of the rail. The bird started squawking, cackling, and ruffling its feathers. It did NOT like my worship music. I was a little indignant at his protest. How dare this crow harass me! I started proclaiming the name of Jesus. The crow began backing up at my words. The name of Jesus is powerful!

"What now, God?" I asked.

"Wait," so I did. I did some "not so" Seal Team Six moves. I texted. I took some selfies.

An older man and woman came up to the bottom of the side stairs I was sitting on. Their presence caught my attention. She handed her elderly husband her cane. She began a slow and what looked to be a painful walk up the stairs while holding on to the rail. I saw a cross necklace hung around her neck. She had a red shirt on. The thought, "That's the blood of Christ," entered my mind.

I heard, "Follow them to the top. They've fought the good fight of faith, and they've been found faithful."

I lagged a little behind because I was arguing with God about being a stalker.

I realized the woman had walked up the steps instead of taking the ramp right behind me. I would have missed her had she decided to take the ramp. The steps were not easy for her to navigate. This was a confirmation for me. I obeyed and caught them both in the hallway.

I don't know where the boldness came from, but I walked up and said, "Hi. I was outside praying on the steps for our state. Praying for some really specific things. I was wondering if you would agree with me in prayer." They wholeheartedly agreed for marriage to be as God intended and to protect life. I asked if there was anything I could agree with them on in prayer. The husband shared his request, "Karen's back has been causing her a lot of pain." We prayed for her back. The three of us hugged and parted ways. I knew in my heart that the mission was complete for the day.

What I learned in Austin:

Had I given into my pity party about the rescinded release or wallowed in my sadness that I would be alone once again, I would've completely missed this opportunity. Things that don't look like they are going our way may be God's setup to witness miracles.

PRAYER IS WAR! Worship makes war without me having to fight in my own strength. Love is war. Worship wins the battle and takes ground for the kingdom WHEN done in obedience at God's leading.

Moment by moment, obedience is key. In my immaturity, I have overridden the cautions of the Holy Spirit. One time, I decided I was going to take my town back from the devil and made some pretty brash declarations. I didn't ask God first. I had a car wreck on Halloween just a few weeks later. This taught me a very valuable lesson: You don't call the enemy into a street fight without getting bloody. By God, if you are warring for His kingdom, it better be because he drafted you. When we've been walking with Jesus for an extended period of time, we learn to be sensitive to his voice. We don't jump into a fight but, if we are put in the battle, we don't back down from it either because the battle is the Lord's.

We keep our eyes on God. We do not jump out in front of him, but nor do we lag behind. We can ask for a confirmation and then MOVE! I don't get to think about it or decide whether I want to do what He asks. I can't take the time to worry about or be concerned I will look silly. If I am thinking about myself, my eyes are on me. If I am worried about misrepresenting God, my eyes are on others. Timing with God is critical. If I'm worried about these things, then I will get distracted.

"You will not need to fight in this battle. Stand firm, hold your position, and see the salvation of the Lord on your behalf, O Judah and Jerusalem. Do not be afraid and do not be dismayed. Tomorrow go out against them, and the Lord will be with you."
2 Chronicles 20:17, ESV

Question

What do you need from the Holy Spirit to have moment-by-moment direction?

Circle one:

A listening ear

An obedient heart

Fearlessness

Holy Spirit direction

Worship

Or write your own

....

EPILOGUE

Well, this is it! You've finished the whole book and are ready for your own Holy Spirit Adventures. The following is some wisdom I've learned while partnering with the Holy Spirit:

1. **Ask God.**
    We've talked about the importance of this. It's a moment-by-moment "asking." Where do I go now? Where do I eat lunch? Someone will come to mind. Do I call them, God? What's next, God? Let Him lead you rather than checking out mentally and going on autopilot.

2. **Surrender your day to Him.**
    Submission to His plans. Submit your to do list. Think about the word SUBMISSION sub-mission. Our plans are subordinate to His.

3. **Learn to discern.**
    Don't be afraid to make a mistake. You will start to see the connectedness. Pray over every place you go. It's hard to describe, but the more you learn to abide in the Spirit, the more you will feel His gentle nudges and learn to flow in the Spirit. Don't be afraid to miss it. That's what learning to discern is all about. When you have the solid foundation of God's written word under your belt, you sense what is of God and not of God. So if you haven't read His word, start there first. When going on adventures with the Holy Spirit, your compass is His word. You can't be led by what you think or feel but by God's word and

His heart. Know His Word, know Him and you will come to understand
what He wants.

4.   **Be willing to get out of your comfort zone.**
            The Holy Spirit will bring His peace, even when you are out of your
            comfort zone. The thing about comfort is we tend to follow the maps in
            our brain rather than trusting God for every moment. I've had the most
            amazing God-led adventures and learned so much more when I'm feeling
            vulnerable and undistracted. Getting out of your comfort zone means
            you need something outside of what you know for help, protection,
            direction. Going on trips alone PUSHED me out of my comfort zone,
            and I saw God do the miraculous because I was clinging to Him and very
            uncomfortable.

The best way to stagnate the waters of the flowing Holy Spirit is to cling to the
rocks of safety in the river. I've been on a leave from the airline, and I noticed
something. I've stopped looking for the adventure. We have to freshly stir
our hearts up and our obedience to commitment and passion as we do in any
relationship.

    I am praying for God to send you on your own Holy Spirit adventure. It's
life changing to experience the miracles that come with that level of trust and
faith. I pray you will be witness to an unseen, but very real God's hand move, and
you will know that you know that you know that the creator of the universe is
pursuing others through you. This is a lifelong Holy Spirit-led adventure. I've by
no means figured this thing out. I'm still learning to let go and listen even today.
It's easier said than done, but basically—you go where He goes. You move when
He says move. You align yourself with the heart and truth of His word. If you do
these things, you are submitted and surrendered to His lead, and I promise you
will be led by the Holy Spirit.